NO-LIMIT
Texas Hold'em

NO-LIMIT
Texas Hold'em

A COMPLETE COURSE

ANGEL LARGAY

ECW Press

Copyright © Angel Largay, 2006

Published by ECW PRESS
2120 Queen Street East, Suite 200, Toronto, Ontario, Canada M4E 1E2

LIBRARY AND ARCHIVES CANADA CATALOGUING IN PUBLICATION

Largay, Angel
No-limit Texas hold'em : a complete course / Angel Largay.

Includes index.
ISBN 1-55022-742-4

1. Poker. 1. Title.

GV1251.L37 2006   795.412   C2006-903596-2

Cover and Text Design: Tania Craan
Production: Mary Bowness
Printing: Webcom

This book is set in Garamond and Franklin Gothic

DISTRIBUTION
CANADA: Jaguar Book Group, 100 Armstrong Ave., Georgetown, ON L7G 5S4
UNITED STATES: Independent Publishers Group, 814 North Franklin Street,
Chicago, IL 60610

PRINTED AND BOUND IN CANADA

ECW PRESS
ecwpress.com

Table of Contents

Dedicated to my greatest teachers:

My father for teaching me what it is to be loved,
and Na'Le'Na for teaching me what it is to love.

Acknowledgements

When I started this project I had no idea how much went into writing a book, nor how many people would ultimately be involved in it reaching fruition. Thanks to all of you, specifically:

Thanks to my friend Jim Sherwood, without whose nagging it may never have reached completion. That, of course, is in jest. In truth, this book may have never gotten past the "some day" stages without his help. Between editing, allowing me to use him as a guinea pig for explanations, encouragement, general sounding board, buying lunch that one day after he found out I just ate, accepting my teasing as well as simply being a friend, he has been invaluable.

To all my students who have come through my classes in the past year, your questions and support have taught me more than I would have thought possible when I began. To my teachers at the table over the past 20 years who pummeled me and my bankroll until I got it, there have been many more than I could ever begin to name but amongst those who stand out from my early poker days in Alaska:

Charlie "CJ" Jerling, who taught me tenacity.

Black Dave, who taught me aggression.

Dave Templeton, who taught me position.

Jimmy "Mickey" Knix, who taught me that it's all a 'P' thing.

Perry Green, who taught me that kindness does not mean weakness — at the table or away.

And Stan Goldstein from California, for the one line that changed my game forever.

To the authors and poker educators who came before me and helped me on my way:

Doyle Brunson: *SuperSystem* changed the face of poker books and began the trend of producing poker educational materials that actually taught. David Sklansky: There isn't a professional poker player alive who doesn't owe David Sklansky for improving the quality of their game. Even those who have not actively learned from him through his books have learned passively from him through playing against others at the table who have. Mike Caro: For his many years of effort maintaining and improving the integrity of the game as well as his groundbreaking work on the people aspect of the game. To Alan "Dr. Al" Schoonmaker for his encouragement and to John Vorhaus for his instant responses to my e-mail questions on the whole process.

To Suzanne Searby for her superhuman effort to edit the entire manuscript in record time so I could hear from the publisher what an incredibly clean copy it was. To my publisher, Jack David, for being so supportive, helpful and for having a great sense of humor.

To Larry Stephens and Chris Salum for the many poker discussions which helped me clarify my thoughts on a wide variety of topics covered in this book. To Renee Wexler who gave the manuscript its first reading and feedback. To Dennis "Batman" Fleig for 'getting it' before he ever read it and just because I promised. Thanks to Rick Gadziola, Rob Kelepouris and Brian Petersen for previewing the manuscript and all their suggestions and fixes.

Finally, to Shirley Morrill, whose cherished memory kept me company for many evenings as I completed this book.

Introduction

I want to share an article with you I wrote a while back:

> About a year ago, I was the subject of an interview
> that has never been published; I can only imagine that
> my answers were not quite what the interviewer had
> in mind, and so it was scrapped. I'm fairly confident
> that I know the fatal answer. I was asked, "To what do
> you attribute your poker talent?" My response? I
> laughed. Then I chuckled. I think there was a guffaw
> thrown in there somewhere too, but I can't really be
> sure as I'm a little fuzzy on the difference between a
> guffaw and a chortle. They frowned. This was not the
> response they were hoping for. Finally I collected
> myself and informed them that, as far as I knew, I had
> no extraordinary poker talent whatsoever.
>
> Aren't you glad you're reading this article now? I
> mean, here's a guy with no poker talent whatsoever
> who's going to be bringing his ideas about poker to

you. What makes me think I can deliver anything worth reading? Good question, and for the answer let's pick up where we left off in the interview process. . . .

"Angel, you've made a living playing cash games for over 10 years; how can you say you have no talent?"

"You want talent," I told them, "there are some incredibly talented players in the pit right now blowing hundreds of thousands of dollars of poker winnings on craps and roulette. Some are at the bar. Quite a few are in the sports book making ridiculously large wagers trying to somehow, miraculously, fade the juice. Go talk to them if you want talent."

They frowned again. "So what do you attribute your success to over the past 10 or 15 years?"

I told them it was a secret. They were not amused. I was amused though, and that's what really counts, so I got busy chuckling and then filled them in on the secret that they found unfit to print — and now I'll fill you in, assuming that my publisher decides to print this.

I wanted it bad. I wanted it really bad. Wanting it really bad wasn't enough in and of itself; I was also willing to do what it took to get there. So I worked hard. I worked really hard. My first year as a pro — if that's what you want to call it — I earned $900 for the year. Seems almost criminal to call that "pro," doesn't it? I rented a trailer for $35 a month on a farm a few miles away from the card room and drove a beat-up Escort back and forth every day. I had no electricity, no running water — though there was a cinder block enclosure with a garden hose hanging over the top and connected with the remnants of a clothes hanger where I used to take my showers: outside, regardless of the weather, 365 days a year. I'd take my car battery out every day and bring it in to the trailer so that I could run a 60-watt light off it, then break out the cards and shuffle and deal over and over again — recording the results in notebook after notebook till I passed out in mid-shuffle hours later. I ate nothing but comped casino food for a year trying to make it at $3/$6. After expenses that first year, my $1,000 bankroll had climbed to a paltry $1,060, but I had made it. It was a beginning.

There are thousands, perhaps even tens of thousands, of players out there who have more than enough talent to play poker professionally, but they don't want it bad enough. Poker rooms are filled with people these days who have flocked to the tables, their preparation consisting of nothing more than having watched three episodes of the *World Poker Tour* on television and having bought a really cool pair of sunglasses. They come to the poker tables totally unprepared to do battle, and they are usually soon separated from their bankrolls. They had the same vision I did many years ago — quit your day job and play poker for a living — but they weren't prepared to make the sacrifices necessary. You aren't going to get a job in the real world making six figures without great deals of effort, education, and drive, and you aren't going to do it at the poker tables either.

Does that mean you're going to have to struggle the way I did if you aspire to become a professional? Unlikely. There are resources today that simply weren't available to me. There are books, software, and classes available today that simply weren't there back when. Certainly not everyone is harboring a dream to become a professional poker player; millions of people play poker for the pure fun of it, and to those millions — thank you kindly, and please keep playing recreationally. There are, however, a growing number of people who have "The Dream." If you're one of them, you're probably asking yourself if you have what it takes. For what it's worth, I'm here to tell you that, if you want it bad enough and are willing to expend the effort to get there, then you do.

Three months into this trial, I decided that $3/$6 limit poker wasn't going to sustain me no matter how good I got at it, but I was determined to finish the year and turn a profit. When the year ended, so did my first foray into professional poker. I had found my calling; there was no longer any doubt what I wanted to be when I grew up. I decided that, if I was going to make it, I would have to play in a bigger game, and to do that I would need a bigger bankroll. That meant going back to work. I was in California at the time and discovered that there were more than a couple of private games back home in Alaska. Funny that I had to go to California to find out where to play back home, but the plan started taking shape. I would go home, get a job, and play poker on the side. I'd build my bankroll until I could quit my job and play full time. How long could it take?

I arrived back in Alaska, plan in hand, and promptly got a job driving a taxi. I checked out some of the games in town and discovered that, though some limit poker did exist, it was a pot-limit kind of town. No problem; how much different could it be? I drove my cab 12 hours a day and then headed over to the poker game with my daily bread. The only positive thing I can say about those days is that I got plenty of sleep. I was usually broke and home in bed in no time. This wasn't working.

Shortly thereafter, I got offered a job dealing poker at one of the games. The pay was fantastic: $20/hour and tips, which figured to be about $60/hour. Now, $80/hour should have built a bankroll quickly, but there was a catch. The nature of the game was that a dealer dealt for an hour and then, if there was a seat open, had to play for an hour — with his own money. I was losing more than I was winning at first, but I came to think of it as on-the-job training. It was a long journeymanship; my training lasted five years.

Once upon a time, Alaska had the best games in the world. Folks who aren't quite qualified to work at a convenience store today were bringing home thousands of dollars a week then due to the pipeline. As the oil money began to dry up and the oil companies started to cut back, there was less and less dead money in the games. I showed up just as the change began and over the next five years found myself, unbeknownst to me, facing tougher and tougher competition. Although I was winning consistently by this time, the amount I was winning was actually quite frustrating. Despite an incredible amount of studying and effort, I was not making anywhere near the money I had expected and was losing hope. Then I decided to take a short weekend trip to Vegas.

I was pretty nervous sitting down to play poker in Vegas for the first time. I told them right off I was from Alaska and immediately regretted it. These guys were waiting for someone like me, some tourist who was going to be easy pickings. Then an odd thing happened. I won. Then another odd thing happened. I started noticing that they were making mistakes. I decided that this tough Vegas crowd was setting me up and was going to move in for the kill at any moment. I destroyed the game on Saturday, making $1,700 in a $10/$20 limit game. I came back on Sunday and reminded them that I was going home the next day. I was curious to see if their play would change. It didn't, and I picked up another $1,200. I flew back to Alaska and stopped at the travel agent to book another trip two weeks from then before I even got home.

My next trip was nearly as profitable as the first. A few of the locals remembered me and didn't give me nearly as much action this time around. I played with a couple of local pros who seemed to be talking to me on almost an egalitarian level. Eventually they got around to asking me if I knew or had ever played with certain players they knew were from Alaska. I responded a bit too matter of factly that I did and that I played with them regularly. "Do you have any idea how good so and so is," they asked? I didn't, but I was starting to get the idea that I might be better than I'd thought.

I spent the next few years playing in Alaska, with frequent trips to California and Las Vegas. As the games in Alaska became less frequent, I decided that it was time to take the plunge and moved to Los Angeles, where the best poker action in the world lives. There I settled in to a $40/$80 limit game and found that at this level the skills I'd picked up playing pot-limit weren't carrying over quite as well as they were in the $10/$20 and $20/$40 games. I was still winning, but I would have to go back to school.

I was fortunate at this point to be playing with a couple

of the best limit hold'em players in the world and learned quite a bit from them as they generously beat my brains in day after day. Also fortunate was that California has some of the biggest whales in existence, and they allowed me to keep my head above water during the early days of my return to full-time limit poker. I did a lot of traveling during the next few years, playing poker as I went. New Orleans, Biloxi, Phoenix, San Diego, San Francisco, Chicago, and more, the games being more or less the same wherever I ended up. I eventually headed back to Los Angeles and southern California, where I comfortably and quietly beat the games for years — till a fateful trip to Las Vegas.

While in Vegas to help a friend out for a couple of weeks, I was approached about the prospect of opening a poker school. Seems they asked around, and my name came up. The folks wanted to know if I'd be interested in developing a curriculum and teaching hold'em. Sounded like fun. What it didn't sound like and should have was work. What followed was the busiest and most hectic year and a half of my life. I developed almost 1,000 pages of curriculum and about 150 hours of classroom instruction. In a nine-month period, I had about 1,000 students, from three countries and dozens of states, come through my classes, and I didn't have a day off for the entire nine months. While it was an incredible amount of work, it was fun, and from that experience came this book as well as the material for two future books, which will be coming to you soon.

The Low-Limit No-Limit Game

While the proliferation of new poker books has been unprecedented in the past couple of years, the poker canon fails to address the actual game that is fueling the poker explosion. This game is low-limit no-limit (LLNL), and it refers to a very special form of no-limit in which there is a maximum amount that you can buy-in. Casinos typically refer to this game as no-limit, but in fact it is a very special form that can't be successfully addressed in the same way as a traditional no-limit game. The game plays so much differently than traditional no-limit that you might do well to consider it a unique structure.

One reason there is so little material written on this particular form of poker despite its explosive popularity is that few professionals have taken to the game. The reason is twofold.

1. The game simply appears too small, and frankly the egos of many expert players demand that they play in a larger game. I know you have watched poker on television and find it hard to believe that some professional poker players have oversized egos, but you'll have to trust me on this one.

2. Those experts who have decided to give this game a shot have discovered that their expert no-limit skills are not completely portable to a LLNL. Many expert players come to a LLNL table armed with their regular no-limit skills and, making no adjustments, walk away disillusioned.

Let's look at the size of the game first. Many of the games we will be addressing have buy-ins that range from as little as $40 to a maximum of $100 or even less[1] — they often have the same amount of chips on the table as you might find in a typical $2/$4 limit game. In fact, I have often observed players signing up for a seat putting themselves on both the $2/$4 limit and the $1/$2 no-limit lists simultaneously. Just as Lee Jones's book *Winning Low Limit Hold'em* recognized the need for a book that addressed the specific strategies necessary to beat the no fold'em hold'em games, there are specific strategies for beating a no-limit game played by the same players.

Yet the appearance of this as a small game is very deceptive. What could an expert player expect to win in a $2/$4 game? Typically expectation in a limit game is referred to by the number of big bets per hour that, on average, a player wins. An expert limit player might win as many as two or three big bets per hour over time if he opts to play in such a small game. However, for the expert player, this would not optimize his earning potential. It would usually be a much better decision to take those expert skills to a larger game even if doing so meant that he would win only one big bet an hour. For instance, winning three big bets per hour in a $2/$4 game would yield $12/hour, while winning one big bet per hour in a $40/$80 game would be worth $80/hour. Clearly no contest — the expert would be better off playing $40/$80.

For the expert player to earn three big bets per hour at the $2/$4 level, his opponents must be making many mistakes, which is almost certainly the case in a typical $2/$4 limit game. When a player makes a mistake that results in

---

[1] *Particularly online games with maximum buy-ins of $50 or even $25.*

the loss of a hand in a $2/$4 game, the mistake usually costs $4.[2] In a low-limit no-limit game, however, because of the no-limit feature, a similar mistake tends to cost the player all his chips. Three such mistakes in a $2/$4 limit game can account for winning three big bets per hour for the skillful player, but the same three mistakes in a LLNL game can and often do result in the expert player busting his opponent, often for $40 or more each time, resulting in a potential for an average hourly win rate of $100 or even more.

---

[2] *This is an oversimplification that will be discussed in the chapter on expectation. A mistake is not for the entire value of the bet unless a player is drawing dead. Also, a mistake can be for much more than a single bet. For instance, throwing away a winner on the end would be for much more than a single bet.*

The Low-Limit No-Limit Differences

Structural Difference

There is but one significant structural difference between no-limit and low-limit no-limit. LLNL is characterized by the fact that one can only buy-in for a predetermined maximum amount, whereas in a traditional no-limit game one can buy-in for *any* amount. This may seem like a rather small difference, but the strategic ramifications are profound. Never before in the history of live-action poker has there been a maximum buy-in associated with a game; the idea is revolutionary.

One effect of this maximum buy-in is that often, even when the small size of the blinds is taken into account, the decision is made to call or bet all-in well before the last card is out. There are a number of difficulties the skilled player faces with such a situation. One is that every action in a hand conveys information to a skilled player, and with fewer actions available based on the small chip stacks information can be much harder to come by. Indeed, a poor player can even out the playing field, simply by raising all-in pre-flop, thereby neutralizing the superior player's skills of reading his opponent, knowing where he is throughout the hand, and subsequently utilizing a well-placed bluff or value bet.

Another example of a troublesome difficulty that arises as a result of the maximum buy-in, which is not present in traditional no-limit games, is the limit phenomenon of not being able to bet enough to protect your hand. This problem takes two forms. First, even if it is your first hand and you've bought-in for the maximum, after a pre-flop raise you may not have enough chips left to bet on the flop to make it incorrect for your opponent to call, even with as little as a draw. Second, even if *you've* built up your chips to a mountain, your opponent may not have enough chips left to make it incorrect to call. Normally, regardless of the structure of the game, mistakes are more costly post-flop than pre-flop. This structure often artificially protects players from making those critical errors.

One characteristic of all successful no-limit players is an aggressive style. Another characteristic not often discussed is tenacity. I win my fair share of traditional no-limit pots on the flop because I bet the flop aggressively, but I win *more* than my fair share of pots on the flop because opponents who might call that $75 bet on the flop understand that I will make it $300 on the turn. In a game in which the maximum buy-in is $100, opponents need not fear a turn bet simply because they will have no chips left for me to attack.

Nonstructural Differences

It has been said that you make money at the poker table based not on your own brilliance but on the mistakes of your opponents. While this is true as far as it goes, a more accurate statement might be that you make money at the poker table based on the gap between your abilities and the abilities of your opponents. Nowhere is this gap more pronounced than when the expert player sits down at a low-limit no-limit table. While this gap may be equally pronounced when an expert limit player sits down to a $2/$4 limit table, his expectation based on the size of the stakes is inconsequential, and he would be far better off taking his expert limit skills to a larger game. This is simply not the case in low-limit no-limit. Here, because of the no-limit feature, one's expectation, even in a $1/$2 blind game, can reach $100/hour or more. The second reason is simply a corollary of the first. Just as inexperienced players flock to the LLNL games, so too do expert players flee them.

If you have the skills or are willing to develop the skills necessary to play this structure, then it would be a grievous error to pass it up. Not only are the financial rewards superior to any game requiring a bankroll of comparable size, but the fluctuations are also the lowest. And the game is simply more fun.

Chapter 1

Basics and Review

This chapter is designed primarily for those players who are new to poker in general or Texas Hold'em in particular. That said, a complete foundation is summarized in this chapter, and I would suggest that even experienced players take the time to review its contents. While some information will seem absurdly simple, even the experienced player may find some valuable tidbits in here. I have three reasons for believing so.

First, I regularly teach classes on Texas Hold'em in Las Vegas, and, while there is a charge for each of the eight 15-hour classes available, I have a four-hour introductory class that I teach free of charge. Many experienced players have come to the introductory class with the sound idea in mind of discovering whether I can teach them something before they invest any money in one of the more advanced classes. After all, you can be an expert in your field and an abysmal instructor in that field; proficiency in a field doesn't mean that you can teach it well. I have been pleased, and to be honest a little surprised, to hear from many of the experienced players, including some semi-pros, that they have learned things in my introductory class that somehow were missed in their prior poker education.

Second, I have found that many people fail to understand some of the most basic strategies, rules, and etiquette of our game even while playing in limit games as high as $40/$80 or in no-limit games as high as $10/$20. In many cases, these players began their poker careers at higher limits based on their economic status and failed to learn many of the basics that those who start at the bottom have picked up.

And third, much of the information I have included here would not have been my first choice if I had written this book many years ago. I have had about a thousand students pass through my school to date, and I have learned much more than I anticipated when I began. There are things I took for granted and subjects I glossed over, never expecting that students would struggle with them. This chapter addresses topics they have struggled with and questions I have answered, in some cases, hundreds of times. For that reason, I would suggest that even the advanced player take the time to go through this chapter, if for no other reason than to understand the difficulty new students of the game face and hence to make more sense of the often hard-to-understand plays they see at the table. In other words, careful study of this chapter will help you to get inside the beginner's head.

If you still believe that this chapter is too basic, then at least do the quizzes. If you ace the quizzes, then jump right ahead to the next chapter, but, if you find that you are answering some of the questions incorrectly, then review the chapter.

Reading the Board

Reading the five community cards (the board) quickly and accurately is a skill, and it takes time and practice to perfect it. Most players don't give the accomplishment of this skill much thought or effort, and if anything players are encouraged *not* to become accomplished at it. A number of students in my classes have told me they originally stopped by the poker room of their choice to get a free 20-minute lesson and were told, right after the lesson, on how much to tip the dealer: "Don't worry about it, just turn your cards up at the end, and the dealer will read your cards for you."

While it is true that the dealer will read your cards for you if you turn them up, it is also true that anyone can make a mistake. The dealer will misread your hand from time to time and even throw away a winning hand. If both you and the dealer are equally skilled at reading the board, I'd bet that you will make fewer errors than the dealer will make when it's your money at risk. Beyond this, how will you know whether to check, call, or raise if you can't read the board with proficiency? The dealer can't help you with that.

Let's say you can already read the board accurately. With the small amount of practice they get merely by sitting around the table playing, most players manage to do so with a reasonable amount of accuracy within a few weeks. Accuracy by itself is not enough; reading the board must be done quickly, at a glance.

Go to a card room and watch a low-limit game in progress. Before the flop, all players will look at their cards (if they don't, then put yourself on the list immediately!). Then the flop will come, and everyone will look at the flop. At least half the table will look back at their cards, often going back and forth between their cards and the flop trying to decide what they have. When the turn is delivered, the same players will check out this addition to the board and then go back to make sure their cards haven't changed and to discover how this addition has helped their hands, often glancing back and forth between the board and their cards to figure out what they now have. The same procedure is repeated on the river. This creates two problems for these players.

First, if you can't read the board quickly, then observant players who *can* read the board at a glance will have a great deal of time to pay attention to you as you try to figure out what you have. They will be watching you at the moment of recognition. If the board reads J♦9♦2♦, the turn brings a 4♦, and you are studying both your hand and the board, it's a safe bet you don't have the A♦ in your hand. Conversely, if you are constantly studying the board and suddenly you don't have to study it any longer when the fourth diamond falls on the turn, then you likely have a big diamond. You don't have to study the board because you're praying to the poker gods for a diamond, and as soon as that diamond falls you know your prayer has been answered.

Second, if you aren't able to read the board quickly, then you won't be able to focus on other players who are giving away valuable information about the strengths of their hands; you're too busy looking back at your own cards.

An excellent way to practice this skill and to give yourself an underrated edge over your opponents is to keep a deck of cards handy while you are watching television. It's a safe bet you already know that Bounty is the "quicker picker-upper" or that you can save a bunch of money on your car insurance by switching to Geico. Don't watch the commercials! When they come on, grab your deck and turn five cards simultaneously on the couch. What is the best hand possible? In other words, if you could choose two cards to have in your hand with that board, which two would you choose? Which would be your second choice? Your third? Keep going. How far you go is up to you, but I suggest that you keep going until you can read the board as fast as you read this paragraph. If you are getting stuck along the way, then you should keep going. If you practice this simple exercise during the commercials of a one-hour show once a day for a week, you'll be amazed how far you've come.

While the cards don't arrive five at a time during actual game conditions, this is still excellent practice, much like a batter in a baseball game swinging two bats to warm up. If you can read five cards at a glance, then three will be a snap.

Take the following quiz and see how you do. Examine each board and determine which the best two cards to be holding are, and then move on to the second best, the third best, all the way to the 20th best.[1] To make it more interesting, time yourself. An accomplished player should be able to list the 20 best hands in about 30 seconds.

---

[1] *Often the availability of two cards is not possible due to another player's holdings, but we will ignore this problem for the purposes of the quiz. For instance, in problem one above, the best hand possible is the J♦T♦, which would preclude the possibility of a T♦6♦ existing. In our quiz, J♦T♦ would be the best, and T♦6♦ would be the second best.*

Quiz 1: *Reading the Board*

A♠7♦9♦A♦8♦

9♠J♦6♣6♥3♥

A♣J♠Q♠8♣8♦

9♣7♣7♥T♠T♣

9♥9♦9♠6♣6♠

Q♠J♦9♥7♥5♣

A♦Q♥2♣T♠4♥

5♦4♥J♣Q♠5♣

6♣K♠7♦T♥9♥

8♦T♦8♣J♦9♦

Recognizing Draws

Frequently you will get a favorable flop or turn for your hand, but there is a draw present that makes your hand particularly vulnerable. For this reason, it is critical to recognize the draws present on the flop. Too many players notice that a draw was present on the flop only after they have been raised when that draw has been completed. If they had noted the draw earlier, they might have refrained from betting when it arrived and could have chosen between folding or putting less money in the pot.

There are two main types of draws: the flush draw and the straight draw.

Flush Draws

If two cards of the same suit appear on the flop, then a flush draw is present.[2] If your opponent has two cards in his hand of that suit, then one more will give him a flush.

Any time two straight-flush cards appear on the flop, a straight-flush draw may be present. While straight-flushes are rare, this situation remains doubly dangerous since it also means that a straight draw is present. Straight draws will be covered in more detail shortly.

Often beginning players believe that, if they have two cards of a suit and a single card of that suit arrives on the flop, then they have a flush draw. In actuality, they have what is called a backdoor flush draw, but backdoor draws are usually discounted by winning players unless they are

---

[2] *Three cards of the same suit on the flop can, of course, indicate the presence of a flush. When no flush is currently present, a flush draw is easily present as all your opponent needs is one card of that suit.*

coupled with another strong draw or already made hand. I will address backdoor draws presently.

Straight Draws

Straight draws are more difficult to see for most players because there are so many variations, unlike flush draws that are straightforward. With a flush draw, either there are two of a suit on board or there are not. However, there are many different types of straight draws, and you must be aware of all of them.

There are straight draws in which you need a single card to make your straight, such as if you are holding the K♠Q♠ and the flop brings a T♦9♠2♣. In this case, a jack and only a jack will make the straight. This type of straight draw has many names. You may hear it referred to as a gutshot straight draw, an inside straight draw, or a belly-buster straight draw. This type of draw is much more difficult to make than the next two types.

Some straight draws allow a player to make his straight with two cards. For example, let's say you are holding the J♥T♥ and the flop brings a K♣Q♠2♥. In this case, you can make a straight with either an ace or a nine. This type of draw is referred to as an open-ended straight draw.

One of the most difficult straight draws to recognize quickly is the double gutshot or double belly-buster straight draw. As the name implies, this type of draw refers to a situation in which you can make one of two different straights, both of which require a single card. For instance, if you are holding the J♠T♠ and the flop brings an A♣Q♦8♥, you could make a queen high straight with a nine, and you could also make an ace high straight with a king.

Other Draws

Draws of lesser strength also exist that are worth little by themselves; however, in conjunction with other strengths in your hand, they can often tip the balance from a fold to a call. Among them are draws to overcards and backdoor draws.

An overcard draw is when one or both of your cards are higher than the highest card on board. For instance, if you are holding the Q♠J♠ and the board is T♥4♣2♦, then you have two overcards. If a queen or a jack falls on the turn, then you will have top pair. Of course, there is no guarantee that making top pair will be good if you hit it; your opponent may have a hand that beats one pair already. Hence, overcard draws are not as powerful as many new players seem to believe. There is one other point of interest regarding overcard draws that we should consider. When you are holding a hand such as A♠J♠ with a board such as T♥4♣2♦, you need to be wary of an ace falling since your opponent is much more likely to have entered the pot with an A2, A4, or AT than he is to have entered with a hand such as J2 or J4. As a result, if an ace falls, he is much more likely to have hit two pair.

Backdoor draws refer to any draw in which you must hit both the turn and the river to make your hand. An example of a backdoor flush draw would be a board of T♥4♣2♦ while you are holding the A♦J♦. You can make a flush if a diamond falls on both the turn and the river. The likelihood of this happening is very slim, just about 4% compared with a 35% chance if you had flopped four to a flush. Using the same cards as above, you also have a backdoor straight draw. You can make a straight if a queen comes on the turn and a king comes on the river. The likelihood of this occurrence is very slight, and a backdoor straight draw, like its cousin the backdoor flush draw, is almost never enough to call on its own.

There is no substitute for practice in finding these draws. The following quiz concentrates on the two main types of draws and disregards lesser draws such as backdoor draws and overcard draws. If an example has more than one type of draw present, list them all.

Quiz 2: *Finding Draws*
1. J♣T♠2♣
2. T♠9♣4♠3♣
3. A♥3♦9♦
4. K♣8♠3♥
5. 7♦A♠3♠
6. 6♦7♣K♥
7. 9♦7♥3♣
8. T♥A♠8♣
9. Q♠2♠7♦
10. T♣6♦4♥K♥

Outs

If you have a draw, you must be able to determine how many cards will complete your hand. A card that completes your hand is called an "out." For practical purposes, an exception would be a card that completes your hand yet gives your opponent a better hand. If that card gives your opponent a superior hand, then it would not be considered an out.

I have discovered through the classes I teach that most players have great difficulty in determining how many outs they have. This is a crucial skill to have because the number of outs you have in relation to the size of the pot will be a major factor in determining whether or not to call a bet when you are on a draw. Let's take a look at a few common examples.

Example 1: If you have the J♠T♠ and the flop brings an A♠7♠2♥, then you have a spade draw. In other words, if one more spade falls, you will have a flush. If your opponent bets, then it is probably safe to say that you do not have the best hand now with merely a jack-high, but you do have a very good chance to improve to the best hand if a spade comes. You have two spades in your hand, and there are two more on the board. Since there are 13 spades in the deck, you have 13, minus the four spades present, or nine spades out of the 47 unknown cards remaining.[3] We then say that you have nine outs.

Example 2: If you have the J♠T♠ and the flop brings a K♠Q♦2♣, you have an open-ended straight draw. If either

---

[3] *Since there are 52 cards in the deck and there are five known cards (the J♠T♠ in your hand and the A♠7♠2♥ on the flop), there are 47 unknown cards.*

an ace or a nine falls on the turn, you will complete a straight. Since no aces or nines are present in either your hand or the board, you have four aces and four nines remaining to complete a straight, giving you eight outs.

Example 3: If you have the J♠T♠ and the flop brings an A♠Q♦8♠, you have a double gutshot and a spade draw. Any one of four nines or four kings will complete a straight, and any one of nine spades will complete a flush. In this example, you have 15 outs. Most new players accidentally count 17 outs, which is completely understandable. They simply add eight outs for a straight and nine outs for a flush, forgetting that they are counting the nine of spades and the king of spades twice.

Often students make the mistake of thinking too far ahead when trying to determine how many outs they have. For instance, in Example 1 above, they might say, "If a nine comes on the turn, then an eight will be an out; therefore, I have a straight draw too." While this is true, it is a backdoor straight draw, and while it adds value to the hand, when we determine outs, we count on the basis of what is present on the board at that moment, not on what may come.

As with any situation in poker, you must endeavor to put your opponent on a hand. In each of the following cases, I ask you to assume that your opponent has a certain hand. While putting someone on a hand is usually only guesswork, it is educated guesswork based on his actions prior to and on the flop as well as on knowledge accrued from observing his betting patterns throughout the game. We will work on this skill later in the text; for now, I've put them on a hand for you. The following quiz will test your ability to determine your outs.

Quiz 3: Finding Outs

1. You have **K♣Q♣,** and the flop comes **T♠9♦2♥.** Your opponent bets; assume that he has **A♠T♣.** How many outs do you have?

2. You have **T♥9♥,** and the flop comes **8♥7♣2♥.** Your opponent bets; assume that he has **A♠8♠.** How many outs do you have?

3. You have **A♠K♠,** and the flop comes **J♠T♦2♠.** Your opponent bets; assume that he has **J♣J♦.** How many outs do you have?

4. You have **A♥T♥,** and the flop comes **K♣9♥2♥.** Your opponent bets; assume that he has **K♥Q♥.** How many outs do you have?

5. You have **9♥9♠,** and the flop comes **9♦8♣7♠.** You believe your opponent has a **JT** for the straight. How many outs do you have on the turn?

6. Continuing from question 5, a **6♥** falls on the turn. How many outs do you have if your opponent has the straight?

7. You have **7♦7♥,** and the flop comes **8♦6♥5♣.** You believe your opponent has a big overpair — either aces or kings. How many outs do you have?

8. You have **6♠5♠,** and the flop comes **9♦3♣2♠.** You believe your opponent has **A9.** How many outs do you have?

9. Continuing from question 8, a **7♥** falls on the turn. How many outs do you have now?

10. You have **Q♠T♠,** and the flop comes **A♠K♣2♠.** You believe your opponent has **AA.** How many outs do you have?

Raise, Call, or Fold?

In every beginners' class I teach, I ask the following questions.

"You are bet into, you look down, and you have a great hand. What do you do?"

Their answer is always "Raise."

"You are bet into, you look down, and you have a good hand. What do you do?"

Their answer is always "Call."

"You are bet into, you look down, and you have a poor hand. What do you do?"

Their answer is always "Fold."

This is an incorrect hierarchy of actions. Raise, call, fold. In most cases, unless you have a drawing hand, the correct "order of operations" is the following:

> Best choice: Raise
> Second best choice: Fold
> Worst choice: Call
>
> Or
>
> Best choice: Fold
> Second best choice: Raise
> Worst choice: Call

This is a truism of poker that just about every professional knows and just about every novice does not. It is not a hard concept to understand, yet it can take many years for it to become apparent to a novice player if someone doesn't take the time to explain it. Most players never get it. Although it's easy to understand, there is no doubt that it is counterintuitive. Let's look at an example.

You are playing in a $1/$2 blind no-limit game. You just sat down and have bought-in for the maximum of $100. You're in late position and limp in with the T♠9♠. Five of you take the flop for $2; there is $10 in the pot. The flop comes T♥4♠2♣. The player in the big blind position bets $10, and it is folded around to you. Most new players would look at this as a calling situation. You have top pair, but your kicker isn't anything to write home about. Your opponent could have a variety of hands that would beat you: AT, KT, QT, JT, an overpair, two pair, or a set. Yet you feel your hand is too good to throw away, so you call. You now have $88 left. The turn card comes a 7♦, and your opponent bets $30. You think to yourself that this seven is unlikely to have hurt you, but $30 is quite a lot. You wonder if your kicker is good enough to win, and you worry that your opponent is bluffing. Most players would eventually get around to calling. There is now $90 in the pot, and you have $58 left. The river card comes a 2♠, and your opponent puts you all-in. What to do? The thinking process usually goes one of two ways:

> 1. "I've got to be beat. He's been betting all the way, he's got to have a better hand than I do, but I've gone this far. I guess I have to call."
> 2. "I've got to be beat. He's been betting all the way; he's got to have a better hand than I do. I guess I have to fold."

You have exactly one way to win if you play the hand this way. You must choose to call on the end, and then you must show your opponent the best hand. Compare that version of our example with following one.

You are playing in a $1/$2 blind no-limit game. You

just sat down and have bought-in for the maximum of $100. You're in late position and limp in with the T♠9♠. Five of you take the flop for $2; there is $10 in the pot. The flop comes T♥4♠2♣. The player in the big blind position bets $10, and it is folded around to you. You call the $10 and raise $30.

There are four likely scenarios:

1. You have the best hand, and your opponent folds.
2. You have the best hand, and your opponent calls.
3. You have the worst hand, and your opponent folds.
4. You have the worst hand, and your opponent calls.

You now have three ways to win. Only in the last scenario, when you have the worst hand and your opponent calls, do you lose. About this time in class someone invariably asks, "What happens if he raises?" If he raises, then you have learned two things. First, he's not going to throw this hand away; second, he has a hand that not only can stand a raise but also, he feels, is worthy of a reraise. Against almost all players, I'm going to assume that I'm beat if he raises, but at least I'll know, and it didn't cost me all my chips to find out. If a typical player raises me in this spot, then I simply throw away and have $58 left. Often, if your opponent does call, he'll be too worried about the strength of your hand to bet again, and you'll be faced with the choice to check or bet. If you check, you very well may go to showdown without having to risk any more chips. If you bet, your opponent's thinking process will usually go one of two ways:

1. "I've got to be beat. He's been betting all the way, he's got to have a better hand than I do, but I've gone this far. I guess I have to call."

2. "I've got to be beat. He's been betting all the way; he's got to have a better hand than I do. I guess I have to fold."

Does that sound familiar? The shoe is on the other foot now, and you've forced him to make the tough decisions instead of you. When you raised him on the flop, I said that you had three ways to win, which you did at that point. If you choose to bet the turn, though, you pick up one more way to win this hand; he may reconsider the wisdom of a call and throw away the best hand on the turn.

Occasionally we hear someone say, "Now there's a poker player" or "That guy plays some great poker." That person doesn't mean he sits around waiting for the best hand and then collects the chips; anyone can do that. While I don't hear it much these days, I recall years ago, when someone would win a hand with a very powerful hand such as quads or better, we used to say something like "Wow, you play quads really well" — the sarcastic implication being "Yeah, okay, you won a big pot with that hand, but it doesn't make you a poker player." Poker players learn how to win pots when they don't have the best hand, and understanding the hierarchy of action will set you on your way.

What If They're Bluffing?

I don't pretend to know all the causes of this phenomenon, but mark my words, new and inexperienced players are absolutely terrified that they are going to be bluffed. In one of my beginner classes, during an introduction to pot odds, I use the following example. You have 5♠4♠, and the board reads 2♣3♦Q♠J♥; there is $20 in the pot, and your opponent bets her last $20. The question, of course, is "Do you call?" The answer, which will be explained in upcoming chapters, is that you don't. In every one of my classes, someone has asked, "What if she's bluffing?"

It doesn't matter whether she is bluffing or not. You can't beat a bluff with this hand; as a matter of fact, you can't beat anything with this hand; you have the absolute lowest hand possible. There are other situations, of course, that are not as simple, such as when you have KK and the flop comes A42. Your opponent bets the pot, but what if she's bluffing? Who cares?

Here's some good news: *good players are more easily bluffed than bad players.* Is that not a strong enough statement for you? Here's another one: *if you can't fold a winner, you can't be a winner.*

If that one doesn't do it for you, then your poker education is going to take longer than I expected. There are times when you can and should pick off a bluff. The time is when you have information to support the idea that your opponent is bluffing, not simply because you are concerned you'll look like an amateur if you are bluffed.

The Object of Low-Limit No-Limit

The object in any form of big bet poker is to bust or double through your opponent. In a limit game, when you are trying to win one big bet per hour, winning an extra bet becomes crucial and can be the difference between winning play and losing play. No-limit is not about winning an extra couple of dollars from your opponent; it's about busting him. There are times when a small value bet is correct. There are also times when you should try to pick up an orphaned pot. However, these moments are secondary to your primary task of busting your opponent.

You may already agree with me. You might even be questioning why I'm trying so hard to hammer home a basic truth that seems obvious to you. Most players, even those who agree with the above words, instinctively adopt limit strategies that fail to keep this in mind. As we proceed through the text, I will point out situations in which this primary goal is commonly lost.

Choosing the Right Game

After you've learned and applied the basics of how to play, game selection is the single most important decision that you can make.

Qualities to Look for in a Game
If you are a regular, look for games in which you don't know anyone. If you are a regular, you know the good players. Expert players don't come out of the woodwork very often. If you don't know the players in the game, it's likely that they are playing for recreation and are not taking the game seriously. If you take the game of poker seriously, you generally are around enough to be noticed. I play in Las Vegas regularly, and if I find myself at a table where there are a good number of players whom I don't know, I often tell a joke that only locals would get. If only the dealer laughs, then I'm at a table full of tourists.[4]

If you are a regular, look for players whom you know often lose. Kind of obvious, isn't it? I mention this for two reasons. The first is to offer you a complete list. The second is because it seems, from the games people choose, that they simply don't know this one. Often I find a game in which a number of tough players have sat down in order to relieve the weak players of their bankrolls, but after they have accomplished this feat and have sent the tourists packing they stick around even though there are no longer any weak players left in the game. This is a particularly bad decision when there is another game across the room they could move to that has filled up with weak players.

---

[4] *Or I suppose it's possible the joke wasn't funny and the dealer was simply trying to improve his chances for a tip, but I typically ignore this possibility.*

Look for games in which there is an expert player or two. This one is rather anti-intuitive, isn't it? Expert players are expert because they have mastered the various aspects of poker. Since they have mastered the basics of the game, and since the single most important decision they can make after they've mastered the basics is game selection, they've chosen this particular game for a reason. Find the reason. Watch their game and see who is playing. If you don't know some of the players, watch for a while and see if there is a truly terrible player or two in the game. If someone is losing numerous buy-ins per hour, it may well be the right game for you in spite of the experts there.

Look for a game in which there is a lot of calling but not much raising. These games are called loose-passive games and are the most beatable games in existence. Tight-aggressive play is a winning style, and loose-passive is the opposite. If many players are seeing the flop without much pre-flop raising, then you've found your game.

Look for a game in which some players are afraid of you. As you improve and put these winning ideas and concepts into action, you'll become a winning player. As you become a solid, winning player, your opponents will begin to fear you. Being afraid is not a winning style. Take advantage of it and play with these fearful folks.

Once you've found the game that's right for you, it's time to find the right seat. Mike Caro has often and correctly pointed out that chips flow clockwise around the table. You want to position yourself to the left of loose, skillful, or aggressive players and to the right of timid, weak, passive players. An aggressive player will often raise. Remember the importance of position. You want to know what she's going to charge you to see this flop before you put any money into the pot. This is accomplished by putting these players on your right. Likewise, timid players are unlikely to raise you or in any way take advantage of their position, so give them position on you.

The Game Selection Gap Concept

You make the majority of your money from weak players' mistakes rather than from your own great play; this is a popularly held opinion that is correct as far as it goes. I would amend this thought to *the amount of money you make in poker is based on the gap between your skill level and your opponents' skill level.*

Generally the greater the gap, the more money you will earn. Actually there is a limitation to this idea as well. If any of you have a background in calculus, you might think of this as a max/min problem. If you are an expert player who is a consistent winner in a tough $40/$80 limit game and choose to move down to a $2/$4 limit game, you wouldn't, despite having a greater gap between skill levels, earn more money. You would, however, earn more bets per hour. Because of the monetary disparity between the levels, you couldn't overcome the difference in earnings despite the increase in gap.

This may seem overly simplistic, not even worth a mention. But every day some of the best players in the world sit down with people whose skill level closely matches their own. Many of these players might do better to take a step down in game size and take advantage of a larger gap.

This can be particularly true in a no-limit game. Quite honestly, had it not been for a twist of fate that prevented me from visiting my regular $10/$20 blind no-limit game at the Commerce Casino in Los Angeles, I would never have found my way to the smaller low-limit no-limit games that have sprung up everywhere. While I was a consistent winner in the larger game, my risk was significantly greater, and despite having an enviable hourly rate I found that I earned more in the smaller $2/$5 blind game with a risk that was nearly inconsequential in comparison. I took this one step further and visited the $1/$2 blind games to see what the result would be, and I discovered that, while the gap was indeed larger here, I had the highest expectation in the $2/$5 game.

Chapter 2

Mathematics

Card Odds

Card odds are the odds that you will make your hand if you are on a draw. You will eventually hear someone at the table say, "I had to call, I had a really good chance of making my hand." Unfortunately he is wrong. First, you never *have* to call. There are times when it is overwhelmingly correct to call, but if the average player could simply strike "I had to call" from his repertoire he would be far ahead. Second, your chances of making your hand are never implicitly good or bad. They are good or bad relative to the pot odds you are getting. We'll look at pot odds in the next chapter, but understand that card odds are simply one part of an equation.

Example 1: Let's say you are holding the J♠T♠, and the flop brings a K♣Q♦2♥. There are 52 cards in the deck, and you know what five of them are. This leaves 47 unknown cards that are somewhere other than in your hand or the flop. Eight of the 47 remaining cards will complete a straight on the turn and give you the best hand. Therefore, eight cards will help you, while 39 cards will not. The ratio of the remaining cards that don't help you to those that do tells you the likelihood of completing your hand: 39:8. In other words, you are about 5:1 against completing your hand on the turn.[1]

Example 2: You have the Q♥J♥, and the flop brings an A♥K♥2♣. Of the 47 unknown cards remaining, there are nine hearts and three nonheart tens,[2] which will complete your hand. Therefore, you have 12 outs. The ratio then is 35 cards that don't help you to 12 that do, or 35:12 or about 3:1.

Example 3: You have the 8♠7♠, and the board reads J♠2♠3♦T♣. There are now 46 unknown cards remaining because you have seen a turn card. There are nine spades remaining and three nonspade nines that would complete your hand. Therefore, the ratio is 34:12 or about 2.8:1 (3:1 would be an acceptable rounding for all but the closest of cases).

A common problem that many players have is understanding that it really doesn't matter where their outs are. Students ask all the time, "But what if all my outs are in my opponents' hands, in the muck, or they're the burn cards?" It doesn't matter. If you have 12 outs, then they may also be the next 12 cards off the deck. That is the tricky thing with unknown cards; their location is unknown. Just as you can't place them in the muck, so too you can't discount that they may be the next cards off the deck.

---

[1] *Actually 4.88:1, but in all but the closest of cases 5:1 will work fine.*
[2] *Clearly the ten of hearts would help your hand as well, but it has been counted already with the remaining hearts.*

Quiz 4: *Card Odds*

In the following quiz, use your knowledge of outs to determine the ratio of cards that won't help you to cards that likely[3] will, from the unknown cards left. In each case, assume that you don't currently have the best hand.

1. You have **J♥T♥**. The flop comes **A♥4♥2♣**.
2. You have **7♣6♣**. The flop comes **5♦4♥K♠**.
3. You have **K♠Q♦**. The flop comes **A♣T♥9♠**.
4. You have **K♦K♥**. The flop comes **A♣9♠2♦**.
5. You have **A♥T♥**. The flop comes **K♥9♣2♥**.
6. You have **A♦K♦**. The flop comes **9♠6♣3♥**.
7. You have **K♥Q♥**. The flop comes **J♥T♣2♥**.
8. You have **T♥9♥**. The flop comes **K♦J♣7♠**.
9. You have **Q♣J♣**. The flop comes **T♣9♣4♦**.
10. You have **J♣J♠**. The flop comes **J♥T♦9♠**.

---

[3] *Often it is a matter of guesswork whether a card will help you or not. For the purposes of this quiz, count a card as an out if it gives you top pair or better with the exception of question 10, where you begin with better than top pair.*

Pot Odds

Pot odds are the odds the pot is laying you on a call. In other words, pot odds equal the ratio of the pot size to the size of the bet you must call. The value of knowing your pot odds is usually in helping, along with card odds, to determine whether or not you should call when you are on a draw.[4] For example, if there was $30 in the pot and your opponent bet $10, then it would cost you $10 to try to win $40 (the $30 that was in the pot prior to your opponent's bet plus his $10 bet). The ratio of pot size to cost would be $40:$10 or simply 4:1.

Example 1: You are playing in a $2/$5 blind game, and six people see the flop for $5; there is $30 in the pot. On the flop, there is a $15 bet and a call before it reaches you. The pot odds are $60:$15 or 4:1.

Example 2: You are playing a $1/$2 blind game, and there is a pre-flop raise of $10, which you call. Four players see the flop, and there is $45 in the pot. You are facing a $45 bet when the action gets to you; there are no other callers. The pot odds are $90:$45 or 2:1.

Example 3: You are playing in a $2/$5 blind game, and there is a $20 raise pre-flop, which is called by four players including yourself. There is $100 in the pot on the flop, and the bet is $500 to you with no other callers. The pot odds are $600:$500 or 1.2:1.

[4] *Pot odds can also be used for other reasons: for instance, to determine whether or not a call should be made based on the chances that your opponent is bluffing. In such a case, if there is $90 in the pot and your opponent bets $10, then you are getting 10:1 pot odds. If you feel that your opponent would bluff in such a situation one time in 10 or better, then you should call even if you can only beat a bluff. Typically this particular example is more useful in limit games where the bets are fixed and usually small in relation to the current pot size. In no-limit games, it has fewer practical applications.*

Quiz 5: *Pot Odds*

Determine what the pot odds are in each of the following problems.[5]

1. There was $125 in the pot pre-flop. The flop has arrived, and there is a $25 bet to you.

2. There was $30 in the pot pre-flop. There is a $5 bet on the flop and four callers when it gets to you.

3. There was $10 in the pot pre-flop. The flop has come, and there is a $20 bet to you.

4. There was $175 in the pot pre-flop. On the flop, there is a $100 bet and two callers when it gets to you.

5. There was $40 in the pot pre-flop. The flop comes, and there is a $40 bet followed by a raise to $160, and the action is to you.

6. There was $75 in the pot pre-flop. On the flop, there is a $25 bet and three callers to you.

7. There was $65 in the pot pre-flop. The flop has arrived, and there is a $10 bet and two callers to you.

8. You have posted the big blind of $5. There are three limpers before the button raises to $20. The small blind calls.

9. There was $15 in the pot pre-flop. The flop has arrived, and there is a $15 bet to you.

10. There was $60 in the pot pre-flop. On the flop, there is a $60 bet and one caller to you.

[5] *In these examples, I have delineated between the pot size before the bet and the current bet. Most examples I have seen don't make any such distinction, instead choosing to say, for instance, "The pot is $50, and it is $10 to you." The $50 refers to the combined total of the $10 bet and the original $40 in the pot. My experience with my students has been that, in practical application at the table, they have difficulty remembering to add the bet to the size of the pot if this is done for them in an academic environment.*

Combining Card Odds and Pot Odds

If card odds confuse many players, then pot odds do so doubly. Sit at any table and before long someone will announce, "Well, I've got to call now — pot odds." Based on seeing some of the hands that people turned over after making that statement, I asked 20 people at low-limit no-limit tables to explain pot odds to me. Not at the table, mind you; I pulled them aside and discussed it privately. Three gave me an accurate definition. Three. While it may be true that some feigned ignorance so as not to share their poker knowledge with me, I left the conversations convinced that most, if not all, were not hiding anything; they simply didn't know. Developing an understanding and working knowledge of pot odds, then, can give you a formidable edge over the majority of your opponents.

Most people at this level seem to believe that from the pot odds alone you can determine whether or not to call a bet when you are on a draw. As with card odds, pot odds are useless by themselves. You must compare the pot odds to the card odds to determine whether a call is correct.

For a call to be correct when you are on a draw, your pot odds must be greater than or equal to your card odds. In other words, if your pot odds are 6:1 and the chances of making your hand on the next card are 4:1, then you may call. Conversely, if your pot odds are 4:1 and the chances of completing a draw are 6:1, then it would be incorrect to call profitably.[6] Based solely on the relationship between pot odds and card odds, you can often determine whether it is correct to make a call when you are on a draw.

---

[6] *Actually there are times when calling with insufficient pot odds is absolutely correct due to implied odds. This will be taken up in Chapter 3.*

These determinations are based on those times when you are on a draw, not when you have a made hand already. For instance, if you have the A♠K♠ and the flop is A♦K♥7♦, then you have a hand that in most instances is the best hand right now. Pot odds and card odds do not affect you directly in this instance. They may, however, affect you indirectly. Let's say that your opponent has a diamond draw. Since she is about 4:1 against completing on the turn, you'd want to bet enough that she would get insufficient pot odds to call. For example, if the pot held $30 pre-flop and you bet $10 or less, then your opponent would get sufficient pot odds to call. Many a player has bemoaned the fact that she was drawn out on when in fact she ensured that her opponent was getting the correct odds to call her on every betting round.

In an effort to cut down on the amount of calculating at the table that a player must do, many hold'em books have handy-dandy odds charts in an appendix, giving the reader information such as, if you flop an open-ended straight draw, you are 2.2:1 against completing it. Or, if you flop a flush draw, you are 1.9:1 against completing it. While accurate, this information can be very misleading. If you flop a flush draw, for instance, you have nine outs — about 4:1 against completing on the turn. There are only two ways the 1.9:1 ratio will help you. Either your opponent has gone all in on the flop, in which case you'll have to calculate your chances of completing from the flop to the river, or he solemnly swears that he will not bet on the turn. I wouldn't place much stock in the second way. I have seen even experienced players make calls on the flop with insufficient pot odds based on the erroneous belief that they are getting better odds than they are based on the information in these charts.

Example 1: There is $45 in the pot pre-flop, and your opponent bets $15 on a flop of K♥Q♦2♠. You are holding the J♣T♣. You have an open-ended straight draw; therefore, you have eight outs and are approximately 5:1 against completing on the turn. You must call $15 to win $60, so your pot odds are $60:$15 or 4:1. Since your pot odds are not greater than the odds of completing your hand, you are getting insufficient pot odds to call.

Example 2: There is $25 in the pot pre-flop, and your opponent bets $5 on a flop of A♥9♣2♥. You are holding the K♥J♥. You have the nut flush draw; therefore, you have nine outs and are approximately 4:1 against completing on the turn. You must call $5 to win $30, so your pot odds are $30:$5 or 6:1. Since your pot odds are greater than the odds of completing your hand, you are getting sufficient pot odds to call.

> **Quiz 6:** *Combining Card Odds and Pot Odds*
>
> In each of the following problems, determine whether or not there are sufficient pot odds to call. Although I have given you your opponent's hands in each case, assume those cards are unknown.[7]
>
> 1. There is $100 in the pot pre-flop, and your opponent bets $10 on a flop of T♠9♥2♣. You are holding the K♦Q♦ and believe that your opponent has the T♦9♦.
>
> 2. There is $250 in the pot pre-flop, and your opponent bets $10 on a flop of K♦9♠3♥. You are holding the A♠A♣. You

---

[7] *There will come a time when you will have sufficient confidence in putting your opponent on a hand that you can take his cards out of the equation. This will cause your calculations to become more accurate. For now, however, we will ignore this so that we can work on one skill at a time.*

believe your opponent is trying to slow-play a set of kings; therefore, your aces are not currently winning.

3. There is $60 in the pot pre-flop, and your opponent bets $60 on a flop of **A♦7♥2♦**. There is one caller when it gets to you. You are holding the **K♦Q♦**.

4. There is $240 in the pot pre-flop, and your opponent bets $120 on a flop of **K♦Q♥3♦**. You have the **J♦T♦**.

5. There is $35 in the pot pre-flop, and your opponent bets $25 on a flop of **A♠Q♦8♣**. There are three callers when it gets to you. You have the **J♥T♥**.

6. There is $15 in the pot pre-flop, and your opponent bets $15 on a flop of **Q♦8♣4♠**. There are four callers when it gets to you. You have the **J♣T♥**.

7. There is $10 in the pot pre-flop, and your opponent bets $20 on a flop of **J♥Q♦2♥**. You have the **T♥9♥**.

8. There is $45 in the pot pre-flop, and your opponent bets $5 on a flop of **7♠4♣2♥**. There are three callers when it gets to you. You have the **A♦K♦**.

9. There is $100 in the pot pre-flop, and your opponent bets $40 on a flop of **7♣J♠K♦**. There are two callers when it gets to you. You have the **T♥9♥**.

10. There is $20 in the pot pre-flop, and your opponent bets $5 on a flop of **6♥2♣9♠**. You have the **A♠T♦**.

Implied Odds

Implied odds are defined as the odds you expect if you hit your hand. While implied odds are an important consideration in all forms of poker, their applications are so overwhelmingly important in NL that they supplant pot odds as the dominant mathematical skill. With a good understanding of implied odds, there may be times in no-limit that it will be correct to call a bet and a raise on the flop with as little as one out. It is unlikely that this will ever be the case in a limit game.

Implied odds are actually nothing new; *they are simply future pot odds.* Let's say that you are playing in a $2/$5 blind no-limit game and decide to limp in and see a flop on the button with the J♣T♣. Six of you take a flop, and the dealer spreads a Q♦8♣2♥. There is $30 in the pot, your opponent bets $10, and there are three callers when it gets to you. Currently the pot is offering you $70:$10 on a call, and you have a gutshot straight draw — a nine will give you the nuts. You are approximately 11:1 against completing your hand on the turn while getting only 7:1 on a call. You are getting insufficient pot odds at this time to call, so, according to what we have learned about the relationship between pot odds and card odds, you should fold.

To make good use of implied odds, you must have a good knowledge of your opponents' tendencies, particularly their willingness to call future bets. In the above example, we need another $40 in the pot to make it correct to call. If we could be sure that our opponents would collectively be willing to put another $40 or more into the pot in the event that we hit one of our outs, then a call would be correct. Let's say that the original bettor on the flop was an aggressive player whom we believed had a queen. Would he be likely to bet again on the turn even if a nine came? Probably so. He bet $10 into a $30 pot on the flop, so perhaps he would bet $20-$25 into a $70 pot on the turn, which would still not be enough. Let's say that at least one of the three callers between the two of you was a calling station who would almost certainly call such a bet. Now there would be $40-$50 extra in the pot before it got to you. If you can make these determinations with a good deal of accuracy, then you could make the call on the flop. Instead of calling $10 to win $70, you are now calling $10 to win the $70 that is in the pot currently plus the $40-$50 that would be put in the pot on the turn. You would adjust your odds to calling $10 to win $110-$120 or more if they would call a raise and/or an additional bet on the river. Now your odds are 11:1 or better, and you should certainly call.

There are a few considerations to keep in mind when using implied odds.

1. You must have a very good understanding of your opponent's play to make effective use of implied odds. If your opponent will not bet, or call a bet, on future streets if your card comes, then your implied odds and your pot odds are the same. Since *pot odds refer to current conditions and implied odds refer to future conditions,* then if your opponent will not put any money in the pot on future streets the value of those odds is zero. The current pot odds plus zero still equals the current pot odds.

2. Your opponent may be a very loose player who would be willing to mortgage the farm in order to call

a bet from you on future streets, but if he only has $10 left in front of him then that's all you can get. Always verify that your opponent has a sufficient number of chips left to lose before calling with an expectation of implied odds carrying you through.

3. You must also have sufficient chips left after your original call. If, in our above example, you have only $10 left after the call on the flop, then you could win only the $70 in the pot plus $10 from each of the players who called the turn bet. In this case, that would be a total of $100, leaving you with 10:1 odds — short of the 11:1 necessary to call.

4. Certain draws are better suited for implied odds than others. All other factors being equal, your implied odds go way up in value if the hand you are drawing to is difficult to see. For instance, if you are holding the J♠T♠ and the flop is A♣Q♦8♥, then it would be much more difficult for your opponent to put you on a strong hand if a king or a nine comes than it would be if you held the A♠K♠, the flop came Q♠9♦5♠, and a spade fell on the turn. In the first case, you held a double gutshot, which is a deceptive hand. In the second case, you held a flush draw, and when the third spade fell even inexperienced players were likely to be wary of a possible flush.

From this point on, the quizzes will become relatively subjective. At a basic level, poker decisions are, for the most part, quantifiable. As we move into more advanced areas of poker, there are more instances when subjective analysis is required. The subject of implied odds crosses that line. Because so much of our decision making now lies in our ability to predict what our opponent will do, along with what statistics say the cards will do, answers are no longer absolute. In some cases, the answer is dictated by the math; however, there are other cases in which your answer may differ. Also, we must begin to put our opponents on hands with increasing accuracy. The answers I offer to the questions in this quiz are realistic based on typical player profiles. Your answers may vary and still be correct; however, if you find that you don't understand how I arrived at my answers, or you find that many of your answers differ, I'd suggest reviewing this chapter.

For now assume that your opponent has a specific hand. While it is rare that you'll be able to put an opponent on a hand with such accuracy, it is helpful to do so now to facilitate the practice of determining whether or not you have the implied odds necessary. I have also sought to identify the type of player you are up against, though even within player types there is considerable variance. To prevent confusion, I have pitted you against a single opponent in each example, though you should be aware that these principles hold against multiple opponents as well. Finally, while a live game situation may call for the use of other options, such as a semi-bluff raise, I will address only two options here, folding and calling; choose the best option from these choices. When taking this quiz, concentrate on *why* the play you've chosen is the best play.

Quiz 7: *Implied Odds*

1. You have the **5♣4♣**. The flop is **A♠K♦2♣**. Your opponent is a typical player and has **AK**. You have $500, and your opponent has $500. There was $80 in the pot pre-flop, and your opponent has bet $50. Call or fold?

2. You have **Q♠J♦.** The flop is **A♠T♦4♥.** Your opponent is tight and has **AQ.** You both have $500 left. The pot had $30 pre-flop, and your opponent has bet $20. Call or fold?

3. You have **J♠T♠.** The flop is **K♥Q♠2♣.** Your opponent is a timid but experienced player and has **KT.** You both have $200. Pre-flop there was $60 in the pot, and your opponent has bet $50. Call or fold?

4. You have **9♦8♦.** The flop is **Q♠T♥6♣.** Your opponent is a loose-aggressive player holding **AQ.** You have $250 left, and he has $75. There was $40 in the pot pre-flop, and your opponent has bet $25. Call or fold?

5. You have **9♣9♠.** The flop is **T♣8♦7♦.** You are playing against a typical player who has **KK.** There was $20 in the pot pre-flop, and your opponent has bet $20. You both have $200 left. Call or fold?

6. You have **A♠J♠.** The flop is **T♣6♥4♠.** Your opponent is a typical player holding a **T7.** You have $100, and he has $125. The pot was $15 pre-flop, and he has just bet $5. Call or fold?

7. You have **6♦5♦.** The flop is **A♥7♣3♠.** Your opponent is a loose-aggressive player holding the **A7.** You have $840 left, and your opponent has $950. The pot had $20 pre-flop, and your opponent has just bet $40. Call or fold?

8. You have **6♦5♦.** The board reads **A♥7♣3♠9♦.** Your opponent is a loose-aggressive player holding the **A7.** You have $800 left, and your opponent has $850. The pot had $100 before the turn, and your opponent has just bet $100. Call or fold?

9. You have **Q♣T♣.** The flop is **A♥K♥4♥.** Your opponent is a typical player and has **AK.** You both have $500. There was $35 in the pot before the flop, and your opponent has just bet $35. Call or fold?

10. You have **K♠J♠.** The flop is **A♠J♣4♠.** Your opponent has **AQ** and is relatively loose. You have $150 left, and he has $100. The pot had $20 pre-flop, and he has just bet $20. Call or fold?

You'll note that in most cases you were supposed to fold. While there are opportunities to call that were not present when we were working strictly with pot odds, the use of implied odds is not a license to call every bet.

Reverse Implied Odds

Reverse implied odds apply to situations in which the pot odds appear to be better than they truly are. Instances where reverse implied odds are in effect normally fall into one of the two following categories.

> 1. You have a strong hand that you erroneously believe is the best hand, and as a result you will lose the maximum. In this case, you have misread the strength of your hand and are unlikely to improve to the winning hand.
>
> 2. You have a weak hand that you believe to be the best right now but with which you'll win only the minimum if it holds up.

The first case is exemplified by the case of set over set. Let's say you have 99 and your opponent has KK. If the flop brings a K93, then you are going to lose a large number of chips unless you have an extraordinary read on your opponent.

The second case is a bit more difficult for most players to grasp. Let's say you had an 8♠6♠, and the flop brought an 8♦4♦2♥. While you may believe that you have the best hand right now, if you bet and are called, you can't like your hand. You are beat by either someone who, at the least, has an eight with a better kicker or someone on either a straight draw or flush draw. If she has a flush draw, she almost certainly has overcards to an eight. Let's say you did bet this hand on the flop, and a J♦ fell on the turn. Do you bet it? Most players in this spot will check because there is simply too great a chance that they are beat by either a flush or a jack. What will your opponent do once you check? She will probably bet a hand that can beat you and check a hand that doesn't beat you. You don't make any more money when you stay ahead, but it costs you money when you fall behind.

Often the best solution in the above hand and instances like it is simply to check the flop and fold if you are bet into before you have any real money invested. If you did choose to play this hand, you would have been forced to play it passively, and passive poker is losing poker. Let your opponents win the little pots; your goal is to bust them or double through them, and that is not going to happen with a hand such as this. You simply cannot expect to get paid off by a hand that you can beat.

Quiz 8: *Reverse Implied Odds*

Determine which of the following hands would likely have reverse implied odds and should be folded. In each case, assume that your opponent has bet the size of the pot and that neither of you is short-stacked.

1. You have the **T♠8♠**, and the flop brings a **T♣9♣4♥**.
2. You have the **A♣2♣**, and the flop brings an **A♠9♥6♣**.
3. You have the **Q♥J♥**, and the flop brings a **J♣8h T♥**.
4. You have the **K♦8♦**, and the flop brings a **K♥4♥7♣**.
5. You have the **A♥K♠**, and the flop brings a **7♣8♥2♠**.
6. You have the **7♦5♦**, and the flop brings a **7♣4♠2♥**.
7. You have the **9♠6♠**, and the flop brings a **9♣2♠2♥**.
8. You have the **T♣7♣**, and the flop brings a **T♠8♦9♥**.
9. You have the **K♦Q♦**, and the flop brings a **K♣7♣2♥**.
10. You have the **K♥T♥**, and the flop brings a **J♠J♥K♣**.

Expectation

As in life, every decision made at the poker table has consequences. Unlike life, every decision made at the poker table has a dollar sign attached to it. Decisions may earn you money or cost you money. Mathematical expectation tells us how much money a decision is worth on average. By analysis of our decision making through expectation, we can accomplish the following.

> 1. We can avoid decisions at the poker table that have a negative expectation and lose us money.
> 2. We can choose decisions at the poker table that have a positive expectation and earn us money.
> 3. We can replace many negative expectation decisions with decisions that have less negative expectations.
> 4. We can replace many positive expectation decisions with decisions that have greater positive expectations.

We use expectation throughout life, though we may not be aware of it. If you are job hunting and are offered two identical jobs on the same day, one offering you $32,000 per year and the other offering you $19 per hour, you start figuring out which job has a higher expectation prior to making your decision. Most people would immediately break out the calculator, and their calculations would go something like the following.

$19 x 40 hours/week x 52 weeks/year = $39,520
$39,520 > $32,000

At this point, they would take the job offering them

$19/hour. While both jobs offer them a positive expectation, the second job offers them a greater expectation, so, all other things being equal, they would accept that offer.

We use expectation to limit our losses as well. Perhaps we've decided that a cell phone is a necessary evil and that we must have one. We compare plans and find that Company A has a plan that costs us $50 for the first 1,000 minutes and $0.03 per minute after that. Company B has a plan that costs us $60 for 1,500 minutes. We've estimated that we use about 1,200 minutes a month, so we would break out the calculator again and find the following.

Company A: $50 + (200 x $0.03) = $56
Company B: $60

Therefore, we would save $4 per month by choosing company A's plan and thus take that plan.

Now let's look at a wagering situation. Let's say we are going to gamble on the flip of a coin. Every time it comes up heads I'll pay you $5, and every time it comes up tails you'll pay me $1. Normally I wouldn't take this bet, but I really want you to get this. There are two possible outcomes every time we flip the coin; it will come up heads, or it will come up tails. In other words, it will come up heads one time in two on average and come up tails one time in two on average. Here is the calculation.

(+$5 x 1/2) + (-$1 x 1/2) = $2

This calculation tells us that you earn $2 on average each time we flip our coin. We say that you have a positive expectation (+EV) of $2.

Let's look now at a simple poker example. You have the K♠J♠, and the flop is A♠7♠4♣. You are heads up, there is $20 in the pot, and your opponent bets $20. Do you call? You are about 4:1 against completing the flush on the turn, and you are getting 2:1 pot odds. According to what you have learned about pot odds, you should fold.[8] The decision to fold is based on expectation. A call here, based solely on pot odds, has a negative expectation. To determine how much of a negative expectation, you must do some simple calculations. Since there are 52 cards in the deck, and you've seen five thus far, you know that there are 47 unknown cards somewhere that may land on the turn. Of these 47 unknown cards, nine will give you the flush, and 38 will not. By calling, you will win the $40 in the pot nine times and lose the $20 it cost you to call the 38 times you did not make your flush.

$$(+\$40 \times 9/47) + (-\$20 \times 38/47) = -\$8.51$$

In this case, you lose $8.51 on average every time you call $20 in this spot. You may find it easier to do the calculation this way.

$$(+\$40 \times 9) + (-\$20 \times 38) = -\$400/47 = -\$8.51$$

Clearly $20 is too much to call based on our immediate odds. So what amount would be acceptable to call? This calculation is slightly more difficult but certainly doable:

---

[8] *Implied odds may dictate another decision, but for the moment let's ignore it while we examine expectation.*

(+\$40 x 9) = 38x
$360 = 38x
x = \$360/38
x = \$9.47

Therefore, if your opponent bet \$9.47 or less, you could call with a positive expectation. This is all academic since you'll never actually do these calculations at the table. To be sure, it is simply much easier and faster to calculate the correct action using your knowledge of pot odds. So why am I showing you this? Excellent question, and, as you may expect, there is an equally excellent answer!

Years ago, while reading my first poker book, I came across a passage about Bobby Baldwin that said something to the effect that he went home and planned even more devastating strategies for the next time he played. That confused me at the time. He didn't know which cards he'd get, so how on Earth could he plan strategy for a random event? As time went on, I began to understand. I'd go home and think about the game and work out theoretical poker situations, and as the years went on more and more often I was running into situations that I'd already examined away from the poker table. While you won't actually work out your expectation at the table, it is excellent practice to work out some expectation problems away from the table. Here is a common situation in which some study away from the table could yield very profitable results.

Let's say you just sat down to a \$1/\$2 blind no-limit game with \$100 and are dealt the K♦Q♦ in EP, and you come in for $2. Five of you see the flop that comes A♦J♦T♣, and there is $10 in the pot. A common error that I see new players making is that they immediately go all-in for all their chips at this juncture. Since you have just bought-in, you'd have $98 left. Well, betting $98 into a $10 pot will almost certainly win you the $10 pot, but it is definitely a mistake.

Consider this: the only way that you can be beaten on the turn is for the board to pair while one of your opponents is holding either two pair or a set. If in fact he is holding two pair or a set, he will need one of three, four, or six cards (the T♦ gives you a royal flush) respectively out of the remaining 47 unknown cards: about 15:1, 11:1, or 7:1. Clearly he is an underdog to hit his hand. How can you determine whether you should try to win the pot right now or try for a smaller bet that keeps your opponent in?

In our example, you've flopped the nut straight, and there is $10 in the pot. Let's assume that if you bet $98 you win the pot right there regardless of your opponent's holdings. Let's examine what would happen over the course of 10 trials.

$$(\$10 \times 10) = \$100/10 = \$10$$

Therefore, we know that this action has a positive expectation of $10.

Now let's look at what happens if one of your opponents has A♠J♠. Two pair is insufficiently strong to call $98 to win a $10 pot. As a matter of fact, since you have the straight already, it may be incorrect for your opponent to call even

$10.[9] Fortunately most of your opponents are willing to make this and even more grievous errors at the table.

Let's say you believe that the majority of your opponents would make a call of $10 if they held two pair in this spot. Since their two pair would need to fill up to beat your straight, they have four outs. There are 47 unknown cards in the deck, and four of them will win the pot for your opponent, while 43 will lose him another $10. Let's determine your expectation if one opponent with two pair calls.

Four times you would lose the $10 you bet plus the $10 that was already in the pot and yours for the taking if you had bet $98 on the flop for a total of $20. Forty-three times you would win another $10.

$$4 \times -\$20 = -\$80$$
$$43 \times \$10 = \$430$$
$$\$430 - \$80 = \$350$$
$$\$350/47 = +\$7.45$$

Your $10 bet on the flop has a positive expectation of $7.45. Our expectation for the entire hand has increased from $10 to $17.45. Note that, while both plays have a positive expectation, the play with the higher expectation is the one you want.

There are times, too, when your opponent is drawing dead and you earn 100% of each called bet. For instance,

[9] *It would be wrong to call if you would throw away if the turn brought an ace or a jack; however, if you would incorrectly call off your remaining chips, then he would be getting the correct implied odds to call $10 if he knew that you would. In actuality, he would probably not know this, and his mistake would simply be rendered moot by your subsequent mistake. This happens often in LLNL.*

if your opponent calls you with the 9♦6♦, then he'd have no chance of winning. He thinks he'll win if a diamond comes, but you have even bigger diamonds.

Quiz 9: *Expectation*

The questions in this quiz are probably not going to be done in your head. You should work them out on paper. While you aren't going to be doing so while you are playing, working through these few problems will give you a much better understanding of expectation and the ways in which you can increase your expectation by selecting an appropriate amount to bet. That understanding will give you an edge over those players who decide that this is way too much work.

1. You have the **J♠T♠**, and the flop is **A♥Q♦8♣**. You need to make the straight to win. There was $40 in the pot, and your opponent bets $15. What is the expected value (EV) of a call?

2. You have the **9♥8♥**, and the flop is **6♥5♣2♦**. You need to make the straight to win. There is $30 in the pot, and your opponent bets $5. What is the EV of a call?

3. You have the **J♥J♣**, and the flop is **Q♥6♣2♦**. Your opponent has a set of sixes and is trying to slow-play. There was $50 in the pot pre-flop, and your opponent checks. What is the expected value of a check behind him?

4. You have the **9♥8♥**, and the flop is **7♥6♥2♣**. Your opponent has the **A♣7♣**. There was $65 in the pot pre-flop, and your opponent bets $25. What is the EV of a call?

5. You have the **A♦Q♦**, and the flop is **T♦7♣2♦**. Assume that your ace or queen is good if you hit it. The pot was $15 pre-flop, and your opponent has bet $10. What is the EV of a call?

6. You have **A♠K♠,** and the flop is **9♣7♦2♥.** Assume that your overcards are good if you hit. The pot had $40 in it pre-flop, and your opponent bets $20. What is the EV of a call?

7. You have **Q♥J♥,** and the flop is **A♦T♣8♠.** Assume that you need to make a straight to win. The pot had $90 pre-flop, and your opponent bets $50. What is the EV of a call?

8. You have **K♦Q♦,** and the flop is **T♥9♠3♣.** Assume that you need the straight to win. The pot had $25 in it pre-flop, and your opponent bets $10. What is the EV of a call?

9. You have **A♥K♥,** and the board reads **9♦6♣3♥3♦4♦.** The pot had $90 in it pre-flop, and both you and your opponent have checked it to the river. On the river, though, your opponent bets $50. You believe that you can only beat a bluff and, further, that he is capable of a bluff — perhaps one time in three. What is the EV of a call?

10. You have the **A♥Q♥,** and the board reads **2♣2♦2♥5♣4♦.** There was $50 in the pot pre-flop, and you and your opponent have checked it to the river. On the river, your opponent bets $90. You believe that you can only beat a bluff and, further, that he is capable of a bluff — perhaps one time in three. What is the EV of a call?

Pot Equity

Pot equity is that portion of the pot that represents your expectation. For instance, if you have A♣A♠ and your opponent has K♣K♠, you can expect to win approximately 82.7% of the time. *Multiplying your expected win rate with the current size of the pot gives you your pot equity.* If, prior to the flop, there was $100 in the pot, then your pot equity would be approximately $82.70.

Determining what your pot equity is during the play of a hand can be accomplished with skills we have already covered. For instance, let's say you have the J♠T♠, and the board reads 9♦7♣8♥A♠. You have become convinced through the play of the hand that your opponent has a set. There is $200 in the pot currently. How do you determine your equity? You need to determine how often each of you will win the pot. You'll win the pot unless the board pairs on the river and lose if it does. Your opponent has 10 outs of the 44 unknown cards remaining (there are six known cards and two semi-known cards[10]), so he is 34:10 against to win the pot. Thirty-four times he will win $0, and 10 times he will win $200. We can express this fact mathematically.

---

[10] *I define a semi-known card as one that hasn't been seen yet but can be reasonably accounted for by our opponent's play. Since we have confidently put our opponent on a set, we are removing two cards from the pool of unknown cards. While this may appear speculative, if he does not have a set, then we don't have to concern ourselves that he has 10 outs. If, for instance, we are mistaken and he has another hand, then he'd have less than 10 outs because a set gives him the greatest chance of drawing out on us. Since all other draws would offer him even less equity than what we are affording him, our estimate of his true pot equity will be more accurate with the use of the semi-known concept.*

$$[(34 \times \$0) + (10 \times \$200)]/44 = \$2,000/44 = \$45.45$$

And here's how to determine the percentage of the pot.

$$(\$45.45/\$200) = (x/100\%)$$
$$(\$45.45 \times 100\%) = \$200x$$
$$\$4,545/\$200 = x$$
$$x = 22.73\%$$

Therefore, you have 77.27% equity[11] of the pot, and your opponent has 22.73% equity. In choosing how much to bet, you must ensure that you bet an amount that, together with the pot, exceeds 22.73% of the total. In other words, if you bet $100 now, it would cost your opponent $100 to win $300. He would have to call an amount equal to 33.33% of the current pot. In choosing this amount, you have led him to make an error.[12] If, on the other hand, you bet $50, then your opponent would have to call $50 to win $250. This is equal to 20% of the current pot, and since it is less than his current pot equity he'd be correct to call.

The application of pot equity that concerns you most in this book will be based on your decision to give an opponent a free card. Situations in which it is correct to give an opponent a free card have both of the following characteristics.

> 1. The pot is small at the moment. If the pot isn't small, then you would normally wish to win it immediately.

[11] *100% - 22.73% = 77.27%.*
[12] *This is an error if you will throw away to a bet on the river if the board pairs. Otherwise, implied odds may indicate a call.*

2. The equity you allow your opponent to keep by not betting to drive him out is smaller in relation to the amount you figure to earn in future bets, usually because he has an opportunity to make a hand with reverse implied odds.

Consider a situation in which you and your opponent both have $100 in chips left and the pot is currently $40. Let's say you are holding the A♥9♥, the flop is A♣6♥J♥, and you have somehow seen your opponent's cards and know that he has K♥T♥. While you have the best hand now, if a bet would cause your opponent to fold when he has shown a willingness to go all-in with other than the nut flush, then you would be incorrect to bet. Your opponent currently has three wins on the turn, specifically the three nonheart queens. These three outs, of 45 unknown cards, give him one chance in 15. This would give your opponent 6.7% equity in the $40 pot or approximately $2.67. If you check the flop, you have allowed him to maintain his $2.67, which you would gain if you bet. Your decision to give your opponent a free turn card would be correct if you would win more on average by doing so than you would give up.

> 3 times in 45: You lose your current pot equity of $37.33. - $112.00
> 35 times in 45: You maintain your current equity of $37.33. There is no gain or loss. $0
> 7 times in 45: You maintain your current pot equity and add $100 to it. $700.00

Your expectation is the sum total of each occurrence ($588) divided by the number of occurrences (45). You therefore gain $13.07 in implied equity by checking the flop. Some may argue that your opponent has a greater equity than this because there are two cards to come. This would be correct if your opponent was all-in, but since a bet would cause your opponent to fold on the turn if he didn't make his hand, equity can be determined one round at a time. There are times when you will go all-in on the flop, and during those times you'll want to determine your equity with two cards to come.

Pot equity is a concept not often covered in poker books, but it is an essential concept that will affect our chosen strategy in low-limit no-limit again and again. While the determination of the optimal play will rarely require you to calculate precisely, equity is a vital concept and should be well understood before moving on.

Quiz 10: *Pot Equity*

The following is a very basic quiz on pot equity. It doesn't address situations in which you are giving a free card, nor does it address those times when more than one card is to come or you face multiple opponents. Nevertheless, it remains good practice for things to come.

1. You have the **A♣A♦**, and the board reads **J♠7♣4♦4♣**. Your opponent has **A♥J♥**. What percent of the pot represents your equity?

2. You have the **J♠T♠**, and the board reads **A♣Q♠8♣2♦**. Your opponent has **A♦Q♦**. What percentage of the pot represents your equity?

3. You have the **9♥8♥**, and the board reads **6♣5♠4♥K♦**. Your opponent has **A♠6♠**. What percentage of the pot represents your equity?

4. You have the **9♥8♥**, and the board reads **7♦6♣5♠4♥**. Your opponent has **7♣7♠**. What percentage of the pot repre-

sents your equity?

5. You have the **9♥8♥**, and the board reads **7♦6♣5♠4♥**. Your opponent has **A♣7♣**. What percentage of the pot represents your equity?

6. You have the **J♠T♠**, and the board reads **9♥Q♠K♥2♠**. Your opponent has **J♣T♣**. What percentage of the pot represents your equity?

7. You have the **J♠T♠**, and the board reads **9♥Q♠K♥2♠**. Your opponent has **J♥T♥**. What percentage of the pot represents your equity?

8. You have the **K♦K♥**, and the board reads **9♥8♦7♣7♠**. Your opponent has **J♥T♥**. What percentage of the pot represents your equity?

9. You have the **A♠Q♠**, and the board reads **K♠9♠4♣2♦**. Your opponent has **K♦Q♦**. What percentage of the pot represents your equity?

10. You have the **9♦9♣**, and the board reads **7♠J♥4♣6♦**. Your opponent has **K♠K♦**. What percentage of the pot represents your equity?

Chapter 3

Meet the People

It has been said that poker is not a card game played by people but a people game played with cards. The further you go in poker the more truth can be found in that statement. While the math is important, it can probably safely be said that the top 100,000 poker players in the world have a very similar understanding of the mathematical aspect of poker. So what separates a Doyle Brunson from a typical grinder with a good head for numbers? It's an understanding of the people aspect of the game.

Let's take a look at the following chart.

Limit	Mathematical/Technical Skills	People Skills
$2/$4	90%	10%
$20/$40	60%	40%
$200/$400	25%	75%
No-Limit		
$1/$2	60%	40%
$2/$5	25%	75%
$10/$20	15%	85%

These numbers represent the weighted importance of math/technical skills versus people skills in various-sized limit and no-limit games. The accuracy of these numbers has been verified by the best means at my disposal. I guessed. While it is a guess, I believe it's a good one. What you should note here is that at every level people skills are simply more important in no-limit, and they become more important the bigger the game regardless of structure.

This chapter endeavors to introduce you to the people who play the game. You'll learn what their tendencies are, what motivates them, and how to adjust your play to beat their particular styles.

The Four Basic Player Types

Dr. Schoonmaker, in his excellent book *The Psychology of Poker,* has outlined four basic player types. Not all players fit neatly into these categories, but they provide an excellent place to begin.

The *loose-aggressive player* (LAP): The loose-aggressive player is often referred to as the maniac. He can be the most dangerous player at the table. He can and will either lose more or win more than anyone at the table, though he is invariably a lifetime loser at the game. Although the LAP can come in varying guises, he is characterized by very aggressive betting and raising with few or no standards. The LAP will raise without regard to his cards, position, or opponent.

The *loose-passive player* (LPP): The loose-passive player is often referred to as the calling station. This player is characterized by her willingness to call too often without any regard for the odds. As with each of the various player types, the LPP comes in varying degrees of both looseness and passiveness. At her most striking, this player will call all bets down to the river with no chance of winning and will never raise, even with the nuts.

The *tight-passive player* (TPP): The tight-passive player is often referred to as the rock. This player is characterized by a very conservative playing style. He will play very few hands and raise even fewer. A lifetime loser in all but the smallest of games, this player is content to sit for hours throwing hands away in the hope that AA will soon arrive.

The *tight-aggressive player* (TAP): The tight-aggressive player is often referred to as "Sir." Joking aside, this player is almost invariably a professional or aspiring professional. He is selective about the hands he plays and is extremely aggressive with those hands that he does play. (Note: because of the often fantastic implied odds offered to the NL player, the tight-aggressive NL player will often play looser than one might expect prior to the flop and resort to a more reflective tight style post-flop.)

Adjusting to Player Types

There are two types of adjustment you must make according to player type if you want to maximize your results: *strategic play* and *psychological play.*

While making adjustments to individual players is always necessary, the need is magnified in a no-limit game. Failure to make the necessary adjustments will often cost you a bet in any game. For those who play no-limit, that single bet may be for all your, or your opponent's, chips.

Numerous books do a very good job of telling you how to adjust strategically to various player types. As a result, I won't take up a great deal of space reiterating information that is widely available elsewhere, aside from a brief summary of a few of the more important points.

Sit to the left of the loose-aggressive player so that she acts before you. You'll know how much it will cost you to enter a pot when you do, and you can reraise to drive players out more easily. Don't value-bet marginal hands you normally would since the risk of a raise is too great. And don't try to steal her blinds.

Sit to the right of the loose-passive player since he won't use his positional advantage over you. Don't try to bluff him. This player will, by definition, call anything. Value-bet marginal hands more often.

Sit to the right of the tight-passive player. Like his passive counterpart the calling station, this player won't use his position to his advantage. Increase your bluffing frequency against him. Beware of a bet or raise by him.

Sit to the left of the tight-aggressive player. Don't get involved in a pot with him unless you are holding a great hand. This player is dangerous.

What I'm going to concentrate on in this chapter is the psychological adjustments you should make while interacting with the various player types. Everyone has his own personality and style at the table. I'm not suggesting that you should adopt mine; one of me is more than enough. What I hope you take out of this chapter is a better understanding of what makes the various players at your table tick and how to make adjustments accordingly. You can adapt your behavior according to your own personality and style to make that knowledge work for you. It's absolutely true that — and this is important, so important in fact that I'm going to give the idea its own line —

If you meet the needs of your opponents, they will meet yours.

This is a basic truism of life — not just of poker. Players often think I'm simply being funny when I refer to the table I'm playing at as one big happy dysfunctional family, but it's a lot closer to reality than most could ever imagine. Find out what drives your opponents emotionally and then meet their needs. If your need is for their chips, then they'll happily oblige. The consequence of not meeting your need is that you go away. If you leave, then their needs will no longer be met.

The Loose-Aggressive Player

The loose-aggressive player is addicted to action. This is a common statement and hardly debatable. What is seldom discussed is what drives that addiction and style from an emotional standpoint. The key to adjusting your play from a psychological standpoint against the loose-aggressive player (or any other player) is understanding the emotional needs behind the behavior. The loose-aggressive player desperately craves attention.

While loose-aggressive players come from all walks of life, when I began investigating individual LAPs I was amazed how many of them used to be captains of their high school football teams or belonged to a fraternity in college that specialized in getting drunk or some other such high-profile, center-of-attention position within society. I found it equally amazing how many of them went into unfulfilling, boring jobs upon graduation. Their lives had done a 180° turn, and they played as if they were seeking to recapture their former glory. Coming to the poker table with a loose-aggressive style puts them right back at the center of attention.

Admittedly this is a stereotype, and it has all the pitfalls and problems that any stereotype has. There are loose-aggressive players who don't come close to this profile, and with them you'll have to dig a little deeper. What is important to note is that, whether they fit this particular stereotype or not, if they are loose-aggressive players, they are looking for attention. Let's take a look at how psychology tells us to deal with attention-seeking behavior.

Although we will examine how we can deal with attention-seeking behavior in a healthy way, I'm not suggesting that we use this information in any direct manner — quite the contrary. In studying how to effectively deal with attention-seeking behavior, we can make an informed choice: namely, to encourage that behavior rather than stifle it. Attention-seeking behavior at the poker table leads to a dismally poor, losing style of play. Why would we seek to change that in anyone?

Here are some healthy guidelines for dealing with this type of personality.

1. Remain unimpressed with poor choices.
2. Use a tone of voice that conveys you are in charge.
3. Don't give him an audience.
4. Ignore his behavior.

And here are some "healthy for your bankroll" guidelines.

1. Act impressed with his poor choices (i.e., reckless gambling).
2. Lower your voice or adopt a more passive or admiring tone when speaking to him.
3. Not only give him an audience, but draw the attention of others to him as well.
4. Never ignore him. Instead, if he seems to be slipping or losing focus on his role, encourage him.

Effective interaction with this type of player begins the moment he walks into the card room. If I'm not involved in a hand when he walks in, I will leap from my seat and announce in a voice the whole room can hear that "Dave"[1] has arrived. Something along the lines of "Hey, Dave![1] Get over here, man, this game needs you!" Picture that scene for a moment. What do you see? Anyone not otherwise indisposed turns to see the celebrity while Dave beams. Which table do you think Dave wants to play on? That's right, mine.

---

[1] If your name is Dave and you've played with me before, this is not *about* you. Unless you want it to be about you, in which case I assure you it is.

When he sits down, it's likely to be to the tune of a statement such as "Buckle your seatbelts; Dave is here!" Once again the attention shifts to him. Once he begins playing, notice every time he straddles or raises in the dark; notice it vocally. He is behaving in this manner to get noticed, so make sure that he is. Go ahead and give him the audience that he wants — it only encourages him.

Constantly monitor his condition, because Dave requires lots of care. Something to be wary of with a loose-aggressive player is when he begins losing (which invariably he will). If he hasn't dragged a pot in a while, he may begin to become withdrawn and actually start throwing away a hand occasionally. In other words, he may begin to play better. While money isn't his primary focus, he does understand that winning a monster pot is a good way to get attention, and, if he fails to meet that need any other way, then he is usually capable of playing better. Don't allow this to happen. If he is losing, my comment might be "These guys have you right where you want them, huh?" Try it when he is in the straddle position and, even if he hasn't straddled for a few rounds, watch it happen. Your comment has shifted the attention back to him, if only momentarily, and he will straddle in an attempt to keep the focus there.

When I get involved in a pot with this player, I add quite a bit of friendly banter — "trash talk" I think it's called today. Pleasant trash talk, but trash talk all the same. "Excuse me, Dave; am I to understand that you raised *me?*" As long as I think I'm ahead in the hand, I'll encourage this back and forth to continue. It's a challenge, and he won't back down. Backing down to friendly taunts is losing face, and he won't voluntarily do so. Losing a pot doesn't affect him; losing the exchange does. Let him have the last word. The last word may be vocal, or it may be the last raise. As the exchange continues, the attention of the other players at the table will oscillate between the two of you. Its final resting place must be on him if you have the best hand. Then there are those times when you don't have the best hand. . . .

If you find yourself in a pot with this type of player, you should be in with the best hand. Don't go splashing around in a pot that such players are in; you need high-quality hands to get involved. Let's say, though, that, despite having come in with what you believed to be the best hand and voluntarily having become deeply involved in this pot, you are no longer convinced you have the best hand. While these players aren't known for being easily bluffed, there are things you can do to improve your chances. If I find myself in such a situation and the size of the pot indicates that a bluff may be prudent, typically I will bluff check-raise.[2] Even inexperienced players are suspicious of a check-raise; it means something. Played correctly, the LAP may lay down more hands against you than another player when check-raised in large part because he already has your attention. I'll be more inclined to be quiet and say nothing after I check-raise, maybe just giving a shrug to any questions from him. It's very interesting to observe what happens when you fail to address his questions and don't look at him. Almost invariably he

[2]Not after writing this book, though. From now on, if I check-raise, it will not be a bluff. Please make a note of this if you are a loose-aggressive player who will be playing against me.

will look around the table to the other faces. What he will see is somber, quiet faces, and they're not looking at him any longer; now the focus is on me. The circus atmosphere you've helped him to cultivate has stopped, the game is quiet, the attention is on me, and it's no longer as much fun for him. It's time to get on with the next hand, and mucking facilitates just that.

The Loose-Passive Player

The loose-passive player is frequently referred to as the calling station. The vast majority are driven by a need to get along and avoid conflict. Strong self-esteem and confidence problems are typically present. The need for a social outlet that provides a sense of belonging and friendship is paramount. Actually making money at the poker tables is so far down the list of priorities that it often gets lost even amid the player's own rationalizations.

The typical loose-passive player is primarily looking for a friend at the poker table. Often he has had difficulty beginning and maintaining emotionally intimate relationships. It's not that he is unlikable or unfriendly; in most cases, it's simply because he tries too hard and can't seem to believe that an overture of friendship is sincere when it does come. Picture the stereotypical president of the chess club at school being invited to the coolest party of the year. He will likely feel a bit awkward, unsure of himself, and a bit set up. Even if the offer was sincere, he is likely to blow the opportunity with his lack of confidence.[3]

As with the loose-aggressive player, keep in mind that

---

[3]*Did I mention I was the president of my college chess club?*

this stereotype is not infallible. There are exceptions. A common exception is the player who is just passing the time. For a player whose vocation is or has been very stressful, poker may be simply a means to pass the time and/or blow off a little steam. Identifying this exception is important because this player has none of the emotional needs of the typical loose-passive player. You can identify these people rather easily because they all share two important qualities. First, they won't play with money they can't afford to lose. Poker is an escape from stress for them, and risking money they can't afford to lose wouldn't achieve that end. Second, they differ from the emotional loose-passive player in that they react differently to conflict. Sooner or later a calling station will be told what an idiot someone thinks he is for making such a poor call. While the emotional LPP tends to cower from this attack and tries to smooth things over or justify his play, the player who is using a loose-passive style simply to pass the time will often meet the conflict head on. He may confront the attacker in an assertive manner, or you will see it in his future play against the attacker; he is suddenly playing to win. For this exception, the following strategy is not effective.

General characteristics of this personality type include the following:

(1) seeks acceptance;
(2) avoids disputes and becomes uncomfortable with conflict;
(3) secretly blames others for his own shortcomings;
(4) can be easily influenced;
(5) acts indifferently to the frustration of losing; and
(6) desires praise.

As with the loose-aggressive player, effective interaction with this type of player begins the moment he walks into the card room. Notice him. He isn't confident enough to stand the same level of attention that the LAP is seeking, but he responds well to a quiet personal acknowledgment of his presence. He will likely enjoy an inviting gesture over to your table to say hello. If you play with him regularly, make a point to learn his wife's or children's names and ask about them. A simple "Hey, how did your son Charlie's soccer game go Saturday? Wasn't that the big game you were telling me about?" will do absolute wonders when you face off at the table.

If he is verbally attacked at the table, as often happens to calling stations, step up and defend him or defocus his assailant's attention. In response to a comment such as "How could you play that garbage — geez, 94 offsuit?" I often interject with "94o? That's my favorite hand! Dealer, how come you never deal me a 94?" The focus has shifted away from the one player at the table who can't handle it, and he *will* appreciate it.

Oddly enough for all the bad beats they dish out, calling stations are secretly frustrated when someone draws out on them. Commiserate with them. A knowing look after he loses on the river that you share his frustration will go far in making you compadres. You may find yourself on the receiving end of a bad beat story as they rehash the hand you just watched. Listen and be sympathetic. Shake your head sadly. Wear earplugs if necessary, but at least look sincere. Which reminds me of a story. . . .

I was playing in a very good $2/$5 game in Vegas when I became aware that someone was standing behind me —

not so close as to be on top of me, but close enough to get my attention. I threw away the next hand and stepped back to visit. He asked if he was bothering me, and I assured him there was no problem. I asked him if he was looking to play, and he told me that he was on the list. It seemed as if he wasn't averse to giving me a little more information, so I asked him if he had played this game before. I discovered that he'd played the night before for a few hours after his plane had landed. The young man told me he'd done all right but had lost a big hand at the end, which reduced his winnings significantly. I asked him to tell me about it and instantly made a friend. I mean, it's not every day someone comes up to you and actually *asks* you to tell him a bad beat story, right? So he delves into the "Story of the Terrible Suckout," and I listen, enraptured by his tale of a travesty of poker justice because, of course, I've never heard a poker story like this one before.[4] I listened intently and groaned at all the appropriate spots. Truth be told, I *was* enraptured. While he described a hand in which he had in fact been drawn out on, he'd played it incorrectly on every street and had given his opponent the correct odds to draw out on him. I was able to learn quite a bit about my new friend before I played with him.

Fifteen minutes later he got called for our game, and I welcomed him and introduced him around the table. He'd become lucky out the gate and had built up his chip stack to $800; I had him covered. Thirty minutes after he sat down, the following hand came up: I was dealt AK under-the-gun, and our hero was on the button. I limped, and

[4] *Yes, that was sarcasm.*

five of us saw the flop. The flop came K♠9♦8♣. I bet $25, and the new player was my only caller. The turn brought the K♥. There was $75 in the pot, and if anyone looked as if he might be willing to call an oversized bet he did. I didn't want to risk losing him, though, and settled on $125. He called instantly. The river brought a 6♥, and while I brought my hand back to reach for chips he went for his stack. He was going to raise. I considered for a moment and checked. He bet $500. He was a calling station, so he could have been on a draw, but drawing for a straight after the board paired and I made a bet almost twice the size of the pot on the turn seemed like such a terrible play that he might have at least *thought* about it for a moment before he called that bet, but he didn't. He called instantly. Another possibility that I considered was that he had pocket sixes and made a full house. Actually that seemed to me to be the likeliest of the aforementioned possibilities. I discounted the idea that he had slow-played me because LPPs don't often slow-play. People don't like it when they get outmaneuvered at the poker table, and LPPs don't want to risk alienating someone. Normally I could have thrown the hand away with little difficulty, but a real possibility was that he might have a king as well with a worse kicker and simply be misreading the strength of his hand. I looked at him for a clue, but he sat motionless. I separated out $500 from my stack and waited for him to disclose something, but he gave up nothing. I then turned over my king and asked him if he could beat it. He squirmed. Then I turned over my ace. He looked downright uncomfortable. Against some players, that would be enough to call, but not against an LPP. He might have been uncomfortable because he was about to beat me and I'd been friendly to him. I mean, I might not like him anymore if he beat me, particularly if he were to draw out on me.

I was still making up my mind when he looked up and said, "Don't call." He flipped over a 75o and showed me the straight. He had called $125 with the board paired to make a gutshot. That's not the important part, though; the important part is what he said next, and I believed him 100%: "I wouldn't have showed anyone else, but I didn't want to take *your* money."

When you're not in a hand, keep the conversation with the LPP light and friendly. Make statements that include him. For example, "Hey, dealer, when are you going to start dealing Bill and me a hand down here?" LPPs are easily influenced, and the extent to which your influence can drive them cannot be overstated.

The following is an actual hand — really. The game was a $2/$5 blind game, and I was dealt the K♦Q♦ in mid- to late position; the LPP was on my left. The game was wild pre-flop but tightened up somewhat post-flop. Five people, including me and the LPP, saw the flop for $40, putting $200 in the pot. The flop of K♥T♥3♠ was checked to me, and I bet $200. The LPP called, leaving him with just $30 remaining, and the rest of the field folded. The turn came a 7♣, and I bet $600. I knew that my opponent had only $30 left, but he didn't know that I knew that, and there is often a psychological advantage to letting someone think you have $600 worth of pride in your hand when there is no risk. He went for his chips to call. I knew that I had the best hand right then. He would have gone all-in on the flop for $230 if he had a made hand, so he was on a draw. I didn't want him in on a draw because he was getting the correct odds for any possible draw. So I stopped him and said "Don't call" while throwing my cards onto their backsides and showing him. "I've got you beat, save your money." He looked desperate and said "But . . ." as he showed me the Q♥J♥. He had a royal-flush draw and had 15 outs for the pot, 2:1 while getting 21:1 pot odds. It couldn't have been any better for him. What was I to do? There was no way he'd lay this hand down; I mean, even a rock would call here, right? I took a chance anyway, rolled my eyes in despair, and said, "Whatever, I've been drawn out on all day by everyone except you, why not you too? Go ahead and try to draw out on me, then." It took about 30 seconds as he fought conflicting desires to call and to please me, but eventually I won as he tossed his hand into the muck, saying, "Yeah, I guess you're right."

This is obviously an extreme example. The LPP isn't always going to be so accommodating. What then?

If he calls, then there are two possible outcomes. He makes his hand, or he doesn't. If he doesn't make his draw, I turn sympathetically to him and explain that I *tried* to save him money. If he does make his draw, then it gets a bit more complicated. I no longer face him. Any light, friendly conversation is over, and though I won't be rude I'll simply act in a manner that suggests we're not buddies anymore. The friendship, the camaraderie: this is what he comes here for. This is an unacceptable outcome for an LPP, and he will do just about anything to set things right. Soon enough we'll both be involved in a pot that gives him that opportunity. Conventional wisdom says you can't bluff a calling station; I tend to agree actually. When I bet or raise into him in the next big pot and he throws away, it won't be because he believes I hold a powerful hand and I bluffed him; it will be because he wants to repair the damage that his drawing out on me caused. He isn't thinking about the cards at all; to him, this won't be about winning the pot; it will be about something much more important — getting along. Depending on how pronounced the player's characteristics are, I occasionally go for two pots in this manner before I let him off the hook completely. Once I have won a pot or two back in this manner, I'll apologize and explain my behavior, something to the effect of "You know, I'm sorry about that hand back there. I hope I wasn't out of line. It wasn't you I was mad at, you know; I just got frustrated from being drawn out on all night." It's always okay, and he will always understand. After all, once again, all is right in the world.

The Tight-Passive Player

The tight-passive player is often referred to as a rock. Such players are risk averse and don't like to gamble. Safety and security are their main goals. They are often retirees who are just looking to pass the time. Often they are sullen, and the word *crotchety* comes to mind. While I've never heard it mentioned before, TPPs in most cases are looking for respect along with safety and security. They also tend to have a pretty high opinion of themselves and/or their playing styles. Tight is right after all, and therefore, if you don't play as tightly as they do, then you must clearly be wrong.

Imagine walking into a 20-table poker room about 9 a.m. Only about four tables made it through the night, but the morning players are starting to make their way into the room by ones and twos. At a table far against the back wall, as far away from everyone else as possible, is someone sitting behind a newspaper, perhaps with a sack lunch on the table next to him so he doesn't have to deal with those "incompetent waitresses." You've found a rock.

Most rocks act as if they don't like people. The reason is simple; people are stupid, much more stupid than the rock anyway. Always calling with garbage hands and getting there, always getting lucky. Idiots. As a result, rocks stay away and tend to be unsociable to all but their rock buddies.

Well, there he is, hiding behind the newspaper on the other side of the room, and by now, you know me, I've got to go talk to him. "Hi, John." This greeting is usually followed by a grunt, and the newspaper stays firmly between us. "I was wondering if I could ask you a question." The paper may grudgingly slip a few inches at this request as he eyes me suspiciously. "It was about a hand I played yesterday, I was wondering what I did wrong." Often I get some kind of dismissal at that point, but he may first ask me what happened. If he doesn't, I conveniently don't hear the dismissal and proceed. It really doesn't matter much what the hand was; I just make certain that I'm aggressive in recounting the story. I might start with something as simple as "I was under the gun with AK and raised. . . ."

When I finish my story, he's very likely to tell me that I should never have raised in the first place pre-flop, that these idiots will just call me anyway, that I should always wait to see a flop, and so on. It really doesn't matter what he says; what matters is that I agree with him and thank him for his advice and time. I am, by the way, still an idiot. I have now, however, been elevated to one of the smartest idiots in the room. After all, I'm smart enough to see his poker genius and respect his advice.

Here are some general characteristics of this personality type:

(1) avoids risk;

(2) seeks respect;

(3) sees monsters under the bed; and

(4) harbors feelings of alternating superiority/contempt.

Our tight-passive opponent sees monsters under the bed, in the closet, on the flop, and in your hand. He is constantly afraid of what might come, what has come, and what his opponent may have. When we are bet into or raised, we all harbor concerns that we are beat (unless we hold the nuts), but normally we push the fear aside, choosing instead to employ subjective analysis and logic. How well we play after that is often a function of our knowledge and experience. With the TPP, however, his level of fear that he is beat, or soon will be, is abnormally strong and often overpowers his logic. It is our job to capitalize on that predisposition.

I have already earned a measure of grudging respect from him because I sought out his opinion. It's time to magnify this respect. Here's a typical play that I might make against him shortly after a conversation such as the one described above: I glance down and spy an absolute trash hand that I have no intention of playing. If I note that the TPP is reaching for chips and is about to call, I will grab enough chips to raise. Upon seeing his call, I will stop short, allowing him to see that I was about to raise. If he isn't paying close enough attention, I may even call for time.[5] As soon as he notices, I will mutter, to no one in particular, "Geez, I was going to raise, and now I don't even know if I can call." Then I'll muck. I was going to muck anyway; taking a moment or two to further instill in the TPP's mind that you have an enormous amount of respect for him will pay dividends later.

He is less likely to call my future raises for two reasons. The first is because I probably do have a monster if I have the courage to raise him, and the second is because he doesn't want to lose the respect I have for him. Since I respect him, he has a certain amount of respect for me. I mean, I'm at least intelligent enough to respect him, after all. A typical situation with this type of player is when the flop comes 7♥3♦9♣, he checks, I bet, and then I say very sympathetically, "I'm sorry, I got really lucky." I am basically telling him that I understand he had a better hand than I did but that, by the time I figured out he was in the pot, I'd already committed myself to seeing if I'd get lucky, and darned if, for instance, I didn't hit my set of sevens. If he folds and I happen to have a seven in my hand, then I'll be sure it's my door card as I flash it and send it to the muck. The TPP almost invariably will mumble something to the effect that "I know what you had, I don't need to see it!" in the most unpleasant way possible, but I'll go right ahead and keep showing him a piece every time I have one. If he does call me, then I'll put on the brakes if I don't think another shot will lose him. If I think it will, then by all means I'll fire another barrel, all the time acting as sym-

[5] *I am not one for wasting time at the table. From calling "time" to mucking will be no more than 10 seconds.*

pathetic as I can. If I put on the brakes, I'll probably see the river with him, and when he turns over AA I'll muck and say something such as "Wow, were my queens in trouble or what?"

I'm not at all concerned that this comment will appear transparent. It might to another player at the table, but the comment wasn't for his benefit. I may even get a secondary benefit out of such a comment if the LAP who didn't believe for a minute I had queens is now under the impression that I will make the same play against him. I won't, of course, but he has one style, and he doesn't adapt it to different players, so of course he assumes that I too have only one style.

All in all, you won't be playing many hands against a TPP, if for no other reason than he plays so few. These suggestions don't mean that you need to mix it up with him constantly. You shouldn't. The TPP will normally have a better hand than you when he comes in, and you should be aware of that. That said, opportunities arise, and the suggestions above are designed to strategically position you for when they do.

The Tight-Aggressive Player

This player is out to destroy your bankroll. If it's your son, don't expect him to remember all those sleepless nights and sacrifices you made for him over the years. Even if he does, it won't amount to a hill of beans against him if he's this type of player. Which brings us to the bad news about tight-aggressive players: they are undoubtedly the most difficult players to influence through psychological means.

Here are some general characteristics of this personality type:

(1) tends to see things in terms of black and white;

(2) is analytical, logical, and direct;

(3) looks for weaknesses and attacks; and

(4) is results driven.

You'll note that these characteristics are less emotional than those of the other personality types; this is not a mistake. To the typical tight-aggressive player, emotions are a waste of time, particularly your emotions. He is right, you are wrong. He is strong, you are weak. He is supposed to win, you are supposed to lose. Unfortunately this is usually not just his opinion but fact.

Tight-aggressive play is not normal behavior; it must be cultivated. This type of play is what gets the money. Since it's not a natural style, and the player has spent the time and effort to cultivate it, we must assume that this person is highly motivated to win and to make the sacrifices necessary to do so. The satisfaction of winning is worth the effort to this player. Normally there are other payoffs for this player, though they are secondary. He may enjoy the respect that he earns and the self-esteem that comes from playing better than his opponents.

Those secondary payoffs may be your only chance. Twenty years ago, when I started playing, I approached many professionals[6] and was treated courteously in almost every case. One thing that has surprised me, more so in retrospect than at the time, is that I was never lied to when

---

[6] *Note that almost all professional poker players are tight-aggressive players.*

I asked a poker question of a tight-aggressive player. I've had my questions brushed off, avoided, or ignored, but I've never been misled. This may be a function of pride in knowing their job well or in the respect received, or perhaps they are all just honest folks, but it is significant.

I too have never lied to or misled someone who has asked me a poker question. I give the person my best answer each time. Often the answer is vague simply because the person asking the question doesn't give enough details for it to be answered completely, but it's my best answer nevertheless. That said, I will use it against that person if the opportunity arises.

For instance, a player asked me about the play of a hand I'd just witnessed, and I gave him honest feedback. He was check-raised by a new player, and he ended up turning into a calling station for the rest of the hand. Among the things we discussed about the hand, I told him that I'd have laid down against the check-raise, that the check-raise communicates his opponent has a strong hand and he ignored it. Soon thereafter we were involved in a hand together, and I found myself with nothing and checked. He bet, the field folded to me, and I raised. He looked over at me and grinned. He is a smart player, and I know it crossed his mind that I was bluffing, but he was in a tough spot. If he calls and I show him a hand, then I may not analyze his hands with him anymore since he is obviously kind of mentally challenged, not to mention the embarrassment he may suffer when shown a winner after we just talked about this. On the other hand, this is kind of obvious, and I'm likely bluffing, and he's going to be embarrassed this way as well. As it turned out, he did throw away.

If you agree that I put him in a tough spot, then did you

see the opportunity I gave him? He could have put me in the same spot, not in that particular hand due to the betting sequence but by looking for an opportunity to check-raise me soon after our conversation. What do I do in that spot? I'll be honest with you — not only would I likely throw away, but also I'd probably buy the player lunch. If he starts playing my game back at me, then he's someone who can learn and adapt quickly, and we will both be likely to benefit from ongoing discussions about poker.

Final Thoughts

A professional poker player of some 20 years, and a very close friend of mine, Ed D., has exclaimed in exasperation on more than one occasion, "These people call you when you want them to call you and fold when you want them to fold *just because they like you*." He's right. As a matter of fact, I have heard variations of the following phrase hundreds of times: "Well, if I'm going to lose, I'd rather lose to you than to someone else." Getting your opponents to consider you their favorite person to lose to is a major accomplishment and a worthwhile goal.

I mentioned it at the beginning of this chapter, but it bears repeating: if you meet the needs of your opponents, they will meet yours. More than for any other reason, people come to the poker table to have fun. As a working professional, I consider it nothing more than good customer service to see that my opponents have a good time. I'll tell stories from the poker table, look up jokes on the internet before a session, whatever it takes to make sure they have a good time. Their entertainment dollars could be spent elsewhere. Make sure they keep coming back.

This chapter will make some people uncomfortable. Ultimately what I am discussing here sounds like manipulation, and that word has a dirty ring to it. One definition of *manipulate* describes the word this way: "Getting people to do what you want without giving them something they value in return." Using this definition, it becomes more difficult to call this type of influence manipulation. The vast majority of the players you will meet at the poker table are coming to have a good time and to be challenged.

If you ensure that your opponents' needs are being met,

then you *are* giving them value. If your opponent is coming to your table for a good time, then show him a good time. If he is coming for a challenge, then challenge him. Give 'em hell — but also give 'em value.

Chapter 4

RIF: Reading Is Fun

Reading the Players

Reading your opponent is crucial in any form of poker but nowhere as much as NL. Because the quality of your opponents is significantly less in a LLNL game, someone with excellent skills in this department might make the most of them by playing in a LLNL game rather than in a traditional, larger, no-limit game. Since seasoned players have often learned how to disguise their hands and have learned the value of deception, they tend to make fewer errors in giving away their hands even though their errors are more costly. In a LLNL game, however, you can often put your opponent on a hand accurately or gain some concrete, valuable information in every hand you are involved in.

Reading takes two forms: reading the players, and then reading their cards. These two skills are, as you might imagine, intricately connected. Learning how to read players takes time, experience, and patience. Despite considering this aspect of my game to be my strongest asset today, I was absolutely abysmal at it when I first began my poker career. Learning to read players was my greatest struggle, but it held the highest payoff of any skill I've developed.[1] It's also the most gratifying. There isn't a feeling in the world quite like calling someone whom you *know* has a busted straight draw when he goes all-in and you show down a no pair king-high, winning a monster pot.

To accurately put someone on a hand, you must first read the player holding those cards. Often, while describing a hand, my students will tell me, "I knew nothing about my opponent; I just sat down about 30 minutes before and hadn't gotten involved in a hand with them yet." There is absolutely no reason you shouldn't know something about a player you've sat at a table with for 30 minutes. In fact, you can often know a good bit about nearly every player at the table upon approaching it.

The time to begin gaining information is from the moment you walk into the room. You read people a little at a time, constantly updating your "database" as new information becomes available.

Let's say you just walked in and are immediately directed to a seat at a $2/$5 table with a $300 maximum buy-in. Nothing should prevent you from picking up valuable information as you walk the 25 steps or so to the table. Here are some examples.

---

[1] *For anyone looking to further improve this aspect of the game, I would highly recommend* The Play of Hands *by Roy Cooke. Although the book may not have been written with this idea in mind, it lets you inside the mind of an expert and shows you how to think.*

1. Does someone have $1,500+ in chips in front of him? This is a $300 max buy-in table. Do you expect this person to be aggressive or passive? (Aggressive)

2. Does someone have $40 in chips in front of him? Do you expect this person to be aggressive or passive? (Passive)

3. Is someone drinking or drunk? Do you expect this person to be loose or tight? (Loose)

4. Does anyone appear or sound upset? This is probably not a strong player; most strong players are in better control of their emotions. This player could be on tilt. Would you expect him to be aggressive or passive? Loose or tight? (Aggressive & Loose)

5. What about that middle-aged man with the tie on and his chips neatly stacked in front of him? Would you expect him to play loosely or tightly? Aggressively or passively? (Tightly & Passively)

6. Is he paying attention to the cocktail waitress or the action? If it's the cocktail waitress, he's probably there to have a good time. Would you expect loose or tight play from this person? (Loose)

7. Is he focused on the action even though he isn't in the hand? What type of player do you think this is? (Tight & Aggressive)

8. Is he sitting back relaxed while he's out of the hand watching the action (Tight), or is he distracted (Loose)?

9. Does he have a girlfriend or wife sitting behind him while he plays? Would you expect poker to be a serious or recreational endeavor for him? (Recreational)

10. Is he reading a magazine or newspaper while not in a hand? Would you expect tight or loose play? (Tight)

Once the dealer begins dealing, you must also pay attention. Don't wait until you are involved in a hand! The best time to observe is when you are not distracted by your own cards. Begin by watching the players as they look at their cards.

1. Did he pick them up sloppily only to quickly protect them from prying eyes? If so, then he probably has a strong hand.

2. Is there a high-hand jackpot? Did he look to the board after he saw his cards? Probably he has a pair.

3. Did he protect his cards with a chip? Does he usually? Often players with a good hand will place a chip on their cards to protect it; when they have a bad hand, they don't. This tell is most valuable with the blinds when you are in late position. If no one has come in and you are in LP and the blinds have not protected their cards, it's probably time to raise.

4. Is he holding his cards in such a manner as to throw them away when the action gets to him? Watch this since it's a very easy tell to fake, but, if he consistently throws his hand away after he's telegraphed that this is what he's going to do, then you can trust this one.

5. Did he pause when the action got to him, considering a raise? He certainly has a stronger hand than normal, better than his average starting requirements.

6. Was he talking and suddenly stopped when he got his cards? He probably has a strong hand.

7. Did he continue talking normally? He probably has a weak hand.

8. Does he seem relaxed, or is he tapping his fingers, bouncing his knee, and drumming his fingers?

9. When your opponent looked at his cards, did he suddenly sit up straight in his chair? He liked what he saw.

10. Does he appear to be more interested in the approaching action than normal, looking to see who is calling or whether anyone raises? He plans on playing.

I illustrate each of these in turn in my classes, always to the amusement of my students. Many think that I'm exaggerating, and most think that these tidbits of information are simply too obvious, that I must be making it up. Then they go to the tables. Even experienced players are surprised when they return to the tables; they find that, when they start paying attention, these things become obvious.

Don't worry about your own cards until the action gets to you. Watch the other players; they are all looking at their cards and giving you information. Don't join them. Look at your cards quickly when it comes to you and do the same thing each time; if you are going to call, then put a chip on your cards, look left,[2] and call. If you are going to raise, then put a chip on your cards, look left, and raise. Do the same thing every time with the same speed.

When the flop comes, look around the table. Everyone, including those people who are not in the pot, will be looking at the flop as if it's a shooting star, and they'll miss it if they blink. I assure you, the flop isn't going anywhere. Watch the players.

---

[2] *A main reason to look left is that often a player to act will telegraph his next move, and you may find that you'll be facing a raise from a player who hasn't acted yet.*

1. Glancing at her chips is a sign of a big hand.

2. Looking and then looking away disinterestedly is either genuine disinterest or a sign of a big hand; however, people normally don't look away as if the flop doesn't interest them when it actually does *and* look away when it truly doesn't interest them, so you have to see someone do this only once. If she looks as if she couldn't care less and then raises, you can be certain that the next time she looks disinterested it's an act.

3. If her hands are shaking when she makes a bet, then it's a very big hand. That's adrenaline, not fear.

4. If she freezes when she sees the flop, then it hit her hard.

5. If she stares through the flop, then it missed her.[3]

6. If she starts talking your ear off, then it missed her.

7. Is a player showing her neighbor her cards? Usually this means she's got a real hand, but if she does show the neighbor watch that person. Neighbors tend to exaggerate their take on the hand the wrong way. For instance, if the player is acting very impressed, then it's probably a bluff; if he looks nonchalant, then it's a big hand.

8. Where are her hands while she's looking? Is she holding and protecting her cards or leaving them out there to be scooped up by a dealer?

9. What happens when the flop comes three diamonds? Almost everyone looks back at her cards to see if she has a diamond. No one looks back to see if she has two. You know whether your cards are suited, but, if your opponent raised

---

[3] *Numbers 4 and 5 may appear to be similar, but they are not. There is a difference between freezing and staring through the flop. In the first case, the player's entire body tends to remain motionless, while in the second case she may fidget in her chair or lean forward on her elbows to get a better look at the flop. In the second case, it's simply her eyes that remain frozen on the flop.*

substantially pre-flop and looks back at her hole cards when the flop comes **A♦Q♦3♦**, then she is probably looking to see if one of those kings is a diamond.

10. Is she staring you down? She probably has a weak hand.

There is no end to the information you can get simply by paying attention, but you *must* pay attention. Learning to pay attention is a skill that you can develop, but it will take time, patience, and discipline. You can, however, significantly speed up the learning curve with a couple of simple exercises.

The first exercise is to find the smallest limit game you can and buy-in for the minimum. In California, I have found $1/$2 limit games that would work perfectly; in Las Vegas, there is at least one $1-$3 spread limit game with a single $1 blind, which is even better. Take advantage of this, because I'll never suggest that you buy-in the minimum again; think of it as a novelty. Now carefully watch the players. Watch them pick up their cards; watch them look at their cards; watch them put their money in the pot. When the action gets to you, quickly *pretend* to look at your cards and then act. That's right, don't look at them. Don't worry, you won't be playing that many hands — this isn't about winning or losing today; it's about watching your opponents. You'll probably lose, but you can win. You'll have to pick your opportunities carefully, but they are there. For instance, one predictable tight player has come in, you are in late position, and the small blind is waiting for his turn to throw away. Now may be a good opportunity to raise. If you can get the hand down to just a couple of players, then you may be able to allow sheer aggression to win the pot if it's checked to you on the flop.

Why do I think this will work? Well, among other reasons, I've done it myself. Also, the only chance you have in this game under these conditions is to pay complete attention. People never know what they can do until they are put in a position where they have no choice. Imagine this: you are training for a race. I'm timing you while you run the 100-meter dash. Your times keep improving for a while, but eventually you reach a plateau where you finally decide that this is the best you can do. I suggest one more practice run, but this time we let Killer the attack dog off his leash and set him on your heels. My bet is that your time will improve, the plateau be damned. Your time will improve because you have no choice. You must outrun Killer if you don't want to end up as his lunch. It's the same idea in poker. Your observation and attention skills will improve because they must if you are to overcome the challenge of not looking at your cards. What you learn from this exercise will go with you to future sessions when you *are* looking at your cards.

The second exercise is much easier, yet so many of my students who rush to do the first exercise never seem to get around to the second one. I understand that because, from the time I thought to do it myself to the time I actually implemented this idea, five years passed. The exercise consists merely of this: go and play a session just like you always do, but pay attention and notice just one new thing about a regular opponent. It doesn't have to be anything profound. I'm not talking about something as obvious as "When he turns his baseball hat around, he is bluffing." While that would indeed be a great piece of information to have, it's a bit more than we could realistically hope for. An example might be something as simple and mundane as "Joe raised with AA on the button." When you go home that evening, write it down. Once I began this exercise, I found that, after I had somehow picked up that 400-pound pen that had eluded me for years, I figured I might as well write this other thing down too since I still remembered it — oh, and this too. Since the goal was to discover one "new" thing, I tended to remember more than one play in case one was a repeat. The first year I implemented this, I played just over 200 sessions, and at the end of the year I had 857 individual notes on just 24 players. That's an average of over 35 notes per individual player! Here are the actual notes, from that first attempt, on one player:

(1) limped in with **KK** in EP;

(2) raised with **44** in LP;

(3) check-raised top pair/top kicker on the flop;

(4) limped in with **AA** in EP;

(5) bet out a flush-draw on the flop;

(6) raised with **JJ** in LP;

(7) raised with **AJ** in EP;

(8) raised with **AK** in EP;

(9) limped with **55** in MP (3rd in);

(10) limped in with **66** in EP;

(11) laid down an overpair when he was check-raised on a flop of **JT9**;

(12) flopped a set, check-called the flop; check-raised on the turn;

(13) limped in with **QQ** in EP;

(14) defended big blind against a raise five out of five times tonight;

(15) raised with **77** in LP;

(16) called a bet with top pair when the river made a flush possible;

(17) lost six hands at showdown this session and played next hand every time;

(18) limped in with **66** in MP (1st in);

(19) raised in LP with open-ended straight draw on flop;

(20) limped in with **AT**s in EP;

(21) raised with **QQ** in EP;

(22) raised with **88** in LP (3rd in);

(23) limped with **44** in EP;

(24) defended small blind against a raise four out of five times;

(25) flopped two pair from the big blind and check-raised the flop;

(26) raised with **AK** in MP (2nd in);

(27) raised in LP with a flush draw;

(28) raised in LP with a 15-outer on the flop, was reraised, and he raised again;

(29) flopped nut straight and check-called the flop, check-raised the turn;

(30) laid down top pair/top kicker in MP against a check-raise from the blind;

(31) limped with **99** in MP (1st in);

(32) raised in LP with **JT**s (four limpers);

(33) called a raise in LP with **98**s (two callers);

(34) raised on a double gutshot draw in MP with three players left to act; and

(35) raised with **KQ**s in EP.

Let's take a look at what I learned. If this player raised in early position, he didn't have AA or KK, though he may or may not have QQ. He will also raise in early position with AK–AJ and KQs but will limp with ATs and small pairs. He limps with medium pairs in middle position but raises in late position with them. He will loosen up his raising standards noticeably in late position, raising with suited connectors. He almost always defends his blinds against a raise. He consistently bets or raises when he is on a draw but likes to check-raise when he has the goods. While he likes to check-raise he doesn't like to be check-raised and can often be taken off a hand this way when a scare card comes. He loosens up when he has lost a hand and tends to play the next one.

The appropriate information to list falls into two categories, betting patterns and tells. Tells are mannerisms that give away the strength of one's hand, while betting patterns refer to how bets reveal the strength of one's hand. You'll note that there isn't a single tell in the list. The list is entirely comprised of betting patterns and tendencies. The reason for this is simply because I was atrocious at recognizing tells. As the years went on, I became more proficient at picking up tells, but simply noticing betting patterns was enough to give me a huge edge over my opponents, and it will do the same for you.

Besides the obvious advantages such lists offer, any time you write something down helps you to remember it. Also, when your attention begins to waver at the table, you can remind yourself you must still get your note for the day, and that will help you to refocus. Not to mention that the sheer willingness to do things to improve your game will, in fact, improve your game. Make the effort.

Reading the Cards

Earlier I said that reading takes two forms: reading the players, and then reading their cards. We took a look at how we could begin to read people; we are now going to explore how we can begin to read their cards.

While every player has his own unique style and characteristics, you can start with your own tendencies when trying to determine what a player has. Until you've developed a better feel for your particular opponents, this can be an effective template. You know typical players. Heck, you've been a typical player before. Let's take a look at a couple of examples and make some educated guesses.

Example 1: Let's say you just sat down at a $2/$5 blind game and the player under-the-gun raises to $20. First of all, listen. Did he say anything when he raised? Did anyone else? It's not at all unusual to hear someone say of a frequent raiser "Oh, it's you again!" or a similar comment. If the player is very tight, a comment such as "*You* raised? I fold" wouldn't be unusual. Let's say you don't hear any comments. He may be just a typical player. What would you raise with under-the-gun? Again, this isn't a perfect model. He doesn't have to do things the way you would, but it's a good place to start if you have nothing more to go on. Let's start listing the possible hands a typical player might raise with under-the-gun: AA–TT, AK–ATs, AK–AQ. There could be more; some people will raise with any pair or any suited ace, and we'll keep that in mind. Three people call him, there is $80 in the pot, and the flop comes K♦7♠2♣. The big blind checks, and our hero bets $50. What would you bet $50 with out of our original range of hands? AA, KK, AK? Maybe he's also betting QQ,

JJ, or TT and hoping no one has the king. We can probably safely eliminate AQ, AJ♠, and AT♠. Incidentally, would you bet $50 if you had KK and flopped top set? Most people would not; they would try to set a trap — more on the wisdom of that move in a later chapter. Okay, his most likely hand at the moment is AA or AK with a chance of KK–TT. He gets two callers, and there is now $230 in the pot. The turn card comes a 9♥, and our hero bets out $100 with both players left to act behind him. If you were a typical player and had QQ, JJ, or TT in this spot, even if you would have bet on the flop, I'll bet you'd check now after getting callers. Let's say he has one caller, and there is now $430 in the pot. The river pairs the board: a 2♥. Both players have about $300 left in front of them, and our hero once again bets out, this time $200. I've eliminated KK entirely from the list of possibilities now; almost every player I run into at a low-limit no-limit table will go for a check-raise at least once during the play of the hand. Our under-the-gun player almost certainly has AA or AK. If he is called and shows us anything else, then make a serious note of it.

Example 2: You are playing in a $1/$2 blind game, and a new player comes in and sits down with the maximum buy-in of $200, two spots in front of the big blind. He opts not to wait and asks to be dealt in immediately, posting his $2. The under-the-gun player, a pretty straightforward player, makes it $10, and there are three callers, including the new player, when the action gets to you in middle position. You have the J♠T♠ and decide to call. Action continues around the table, and six of you see the flop. Okay, let's back up a bit. The new player bought-in for the maximum, so the chances are that he is aggressive. He also chose not to wait two hands for the big blind, choosing instead to post; this is loose behavior. He came to play, not to wait. It was raised in front of him, and he called the raise. Well, it's certainly possible that he has a real hand, but it's more likely he doesn't, simply because there are more poor hands than there are quality hands. He likely doesn't have a premium hand, because he would have reraised. Is it possible that he has a premium hand? Certainly, but based on the information we have at hand thus far probably not. Remember that we decided he was a loose-aggressive player. Such players would be even more likely to reraise with any excuse, and a premium hand would do nicely for an excuse. This is not conclusive. We don't know enough about this player to make this determination with certainty, but we must begin somewhere. When you are starting out reading a hand, don't flip-flop without a reason. You believe that he was loose-aggressive; believe, then, that he will act accordingly until you have evidence to the contrary. He may be loose-aggressive and tricky, but wait till you have evidence of trickery before you give him credit for it.

Okay, there are six players on the flop, which comes J♦T♥6♠. The under-the-gun player bets $20, the new player raises to $40, and it's on to you. What do you put them on? There was $60 in the pot on the flop, and the original raiser bets $20. Why would he do that? What could he raise with pre-flop and then bet $20? What would you do that with? Don't think of a specific hand; think of a range of hands. Betting $20 is a weak bet into a $60 pot unless he's low on chips; let's assume that isn't the case. We know he's a pretty straightforward player, meaning he bets when he has a hand and checks when he doesn't. So it's likely that he has a hand but isn't in love with it. He made a probing type of bet to see what he was up against. In our previous example, we put a typical pre-flop raiser on one of these hands: AA–TT, AK–ATs, AK–AQ. A $20 bet doesn't sound like JJ or TT, so let's abandon those as candidates, at least for now; we'll know for sure in a moment when we see how he reacts to the raise, but for now let's dismiss them. We can probably dismiss ATs as well. He's a straightforward player who bets a hand when he has one and checks when he doesn't, so let's cross AK and AQ off the list as well. That leaves AA, KK, QQ, or AJs. The new player raised. What do we know about him? Well, he's loose-aggressive, for starters. Also, he raised the minimum, which is a weak play. His particular style would be to raise anyway, so it's likely that a raise such as this indicates a draw at best. If he had a powerhouse, the raise would likely be larger. The under-the-gun player almost certainly has one pair, which we can beat, and the new player likely has a draw, which we also can beat. We can be relatively confident that our hand is better than either of theirs at the moment. A quick look left should tell us what we are up against with the players still left to act. Do they seem very interested in the action, or are they getting ready to muck? Let's not complicate the hand any further and suggest that it appears they are ready to muck. While I'll leave the play of the rest of the hand for future chapters, after we've added some important principles to our repertoire, you can perhaps begin to see how putting someone on a hand is done. Let's look at one more example.

Example 3: This was a recent hand I played that illustrates a good number of important principles. I was playing in a $2/$5 game and was in early position, three off the button. I limped with an A♠Q♦, and four of us saw the flop. There was $20 in the pot, and the flop came A♣9♥2♥. The big blind checked, and I bet $20. The next player folded, a loose-passive player in late position called immediately, and the big blind folded. An important consideration at this point in the hand is that we both had about $500 left in front of us. Now, what do you think he had? I suspected that he had a flush draw. Why a flush draw and not an ace? I'll give you a chance to answer that for yourself. Assume that you were in his spot. You were holding the AT, and I bet $20. What would have gone through your mind?

A number of things should have, including these starters.

1. What is the range of hands he could have?
2. Do I have the best hand right now?
3. What is the likelihood that I could improve to the best hand if I don't have the best hand now?
4. Based on the answers to the above questions, should I call, raise, or fold?

It takes time to answer those questions. I'm not talking about 15 minutes, but it does take a couple of seconds.[4] I was called immediately. What type of hand takes no time to think about? The answer is a draw. He didn't consider

---

[4] *It has been suggested to me that a calling station wouldn't necessarily have to think about calling — not even for a second. There is truth in that, but a calling station will usually pause long enough to come up with a justification for the call. Barring a decent justification, he will probably still call, which precludes the need for thinking in the first place, but few are self-aware of their stylistic problems.*

what I had because it didn't matter what I had if he was on a draw. He didn't wonder if he had the best hand right then because he believed he had to make his hand to win. He "knew" that if he made his hand he'd have me beat no matter what I had.[5] He didn't think about the pot odds he was getting because he's a calling station, and that goes against his religion. Since he had nothing to think about, he instantly called. The only reasonable draw possible was a flush draw, so I decided that he had two hearts. While it's true that he could have had the A♥, this possibility didn't concern me simply because the only way he could have had a flush draw, an ace, and have me beat was if he had A♥K♥, and he would have raised pre-flop with this. The rest of the hand was inconsequential since it revealed nothing further about his hand. He showed a K♥T♥ on the river as he threw away.

Don't be concerned at this point if you didn't see the trail of logic in these examples. If you were able to follow the logic and understand where the conclusions stemmed from, then you are well on your way to being able to do it for yourself. I've prepared the following short quiz for you to take for practice. In this quiz, you'll be asked to determine what your opponent most likely has. Putting someone on a hand is an inexact science, particularly on paper. A "tight" player, for instance, comes in many shapes and sizes, so you may find the descriptions within the questions vague. What you should keep in mind as you answer these questions is what would cause your opponent

---

[5] *Not necessarily; I could make a bigger flush when he makes his, but few players consider this possibility.*

to act in the manner described. If you don't know, then start by determining why you would act in such a way.

Quiz 11: Reading the Cards

1. You are holding the **AJ**, and the flop comes **A♦9♦3♣**. Your opponent thinks for a moment, then checks, and you bet. Your opponent almost beats you in the pot. The turn comes a **6**s, and your opponent considers and then checks again. When you bet, once again he almost beats you in the pot. What does he most likely have?

2. Your opponent raised pre-flop, and you called with **AJs**. The flop comes **A♦9♥3♣**. Your opponent cuts out some chips, stares you down for a moment, and then, just before committing himself to a bet, decides reluctantly, in a magnanimous gesture, to check. What does he most likely have?

3. Your opponent raised pre-flop, and you called with **AJs**. He proceeds to bet in the dark. The flop comes **A♦9♥3♣**. Is your hand good?

4. You are holding **AJ**, and the flop comes **A♦9♥3♣**. Your opponent bets. You reach for chips to call him, and he looks back at his hand. Is your hand good?

5. You are on the button in a typical $2/$5 game, and it is folded around to you where you find **A♠Q♠**. The blinds are both very tight players. You decide to raise to $20. The small blind folds, and the big blind raises to $75. You call, and the flop comes **A♦9♦3♣**, and the big blind checks. What do you do and why?

6. You are in MP with the **Q♠J♠**, there are three limpers to you, and you decide to limp along. There is one caller behind you, and both blinds come. You take the flop six-handed. The flop comes **A♣Q♦6♥**. The blinds check, and the UTG player bets $30. It's folded around to you. What do you do and why?

7. You find yourself with **Q♠Q♦** in the big blind. An EP player calls, a LAP in MP calls, and an LP player raises to $20. You decide to call, the EP player folds, while the MP player raises all-in to $200. The LP player mucks, and it is to you. What do you do and why?

8. You are in late position with **Q♠Q♦**. The under-the-gun player, a new player who just sat down, makes it $20 to go. You call, and the big blind calls. The flop is **K♠Q♥2♣**. The big blind thinks for a moment and then checks, and the under-the-gun player bets $50. You raise to $200, the big blind calls immediately, and the under-the-gun player folds. The turn comes a **9♠**, and the big blind checks immediately and calls for the cocktail waitress. What do you do and why?

9. A continuation from the previous hand: the river is the **4♦**, and the player in the big blind position bets $250. What do you do and why?

10. You are in late position with the **J♥J♦**. A good player in early position raised to $20, it is folded around to you, and you raise to $60. Your opponent considers and then flat-calls you. The flop is **9♠7♦2♣**. Your opponent bets $125. What do you do and why?

Chapter 5

Pre-Flop

General Pre-Flop Guidelines by Game Type

Taking the template we used to define the four basic player types, we can define basic game textures and change our play accordingly.

If the game is mostly loose-passive: You can see quite a few flops in such a game. If it's costing you the minimum to see a flop, then the implied odds make it correct to see the flop with a wide variety of hands.[1] Furthermore, since the players are playing mostly a loose-passive game, you'll get cheap draws when you are trying to make a hand, and you'll be paid off when you have one. You can and almost always should play all pairs, suited connectors, unsuited

---

[1] *This assumes that neither you nor the rest of the table as a whole is extremely short-stacked.*

connectors, suited gappers, and even unsuited gappers. There are some trouble hands you should stay away from such as KT, A9, et cetera. Being drawn out on in a game such as this is always a concern, but with a hand such as A9 you must also be cautious about the possibility that you are dominated. However, I will often see the flop with hands as poor as 86 or even 74s. While the danger of being drawn out on is just as real, if I hit one of these hands, I am likely to be all alone with it and receive full value out of it as well.

If the game is mostly loose-aggressive: You should tighten up and take advantage of your opponents' loose play by coming in with superior hands. Once involved, though, be prepared for a high level of aggression. This type of game allows for your greatest expectation if played correctly, but you mustn't play too safely; you must get in there and mix it up if you feel you have the best of it. By "superior hands," I mean those that can win unimproved, hands such as pairs or big aces. If nearly every hand is being raised a reasonable amount[2] pre-flop, then I'll loosen up a bit if I can get multiway action on hands such as suited connectors if I'm in late position and unlikely to face a reraise. If the pot is being raised an unreasonable amount[3] almost every hand, then I will simply wait for premium hands. Due to the cap on the buy-in for these games, such a raise is too significant for the size of the stacks, and the

---

[2] *A reasonable raise is roughly the size of the pot. In a $2/$5 game, if the opener is bringing it in for $20 or so, this is reasonable.*
[3] *An unreasonable raise would be twice the size of the pot or more. In a $2/$5 game, if the opener is opening for $40 regularly, this is unreasonably high.*

raisers are forcing you to gamble. If you are forced to gamble, do so with a superior hand. Patience is the name of this game. Don't be discouraged, because when you do come in you'll almost always be a big favorite, and you stand to double up.

If the game is mostly tight-passive: It now no longer matters what you have. You can see the flop with literally anything. I have played entire sessions in a tight-passive game without looking at my hole cards once. This statement isn't meant to be boastful. The important thing to focus on is your opponents. Looking at your cards simply takes your attention away from the most important factor in the game. You must, however, be able to play the players in such a game. Your cards don't matter because you have the opportunity to use so many other factors to your advantage: position, aggression, table image, and so on. If you haven't become comfortable with using these other factors to your advantage, then practice in this game — it is almost foolproof.

If the game is mostly tight-aggressive: Look for another game. Seriously. There's no need to play in a game such as this these days since the LLNL craze provides opportunities to find another game. I suppose I should say something further here, but I'd like to point out first that, in the two years since this game has become popular, I have played it nearly exclusively and have yet to find a tight-aggressive game. If you believe you have found such a game, I'd suggest you look a bit harder at it, since it's more likely that you are giving the players too much respect and perhaps playing a bit too passively yourself rather than that the game is truly tight-aggressive. Let's say, though, that, after a thorough second look and the absence of another game within 50 miles, you've determined that this game is indeed tight-aggressive. Now what? You'll want to tighten up your starting requirements significantly, but when you do come in come in swinging. Don't allow the other players to bully you. The best way to handle these TAPs is to pass more frequently when you are bet or raised into and to bet and raise into them more often. Very good players don't like calling off their chips; they prefer to be the ones doing the betting. There can be an advantage in finding yourself with no options but a tight game such as this. When I began my poker career back in Alaska, I faced some of the toughest players I have faced anywhere. The nearest alternative was over 3,000 miles away, and the commute was hell, so I stayed and played. I struggled, but I learned things in those games that I might never have learned with easier, softer alternatives.

Pre-Flop Strategy

I once posted this question on a popular poker forum: "What would you like to be taught in a no-limit class?" Many of the questions repeatedly asked about how to play or whether to play AK for a raise pre-flop or whether 99 is good enough to raise with, and so on. Unlike limit hold'em, where we can begin to give quantifiable answers to such questions, in no-limit it's impossible. In my limit classes, much time is devoted to pre-flop starting requirements. Correct decisions on which hands to come in with pre-flop are crucial to success in limit. In limit, there is a quantifiable formula for making these determinations that is subject to minor modifications based on particular opponents. In contrast, in no-limit there is very little in the way of a quantifiable formula for which cards to enter into the pot pre-flop. Rather, any attempt to give a quantifiable formula in no-limit is subject to the players involved, and the minor modifications are based on the cards.

In no-limit, there are guidelines, but there is no such thing as a pre-flop requirement. Remember, this isn't a card game — it's a people game. If at all possible, begin studying the people playing in your game before you sit down to join them. Frequently it's not possible, since often you walk into a card room to discover an empty seat that won't be empty long if you fail to take it, but there will be times when you are on the waiting list for a game and have the opportunity to watch the players prior to sitting down. Use this time. Watch the players to learn about them. Who is playing with short money? Who are the aggressors at the table? What are they coming in with? Whom can you push around? Who is going to push back?

While I normally come in with relatively solid starting hands based on the guidelines I discussed in the previous section, everything depends on the situation.

Hand Strength Criteria

There are at least 10 criteria for evaluating the strength of your hand:[4]

(1) your cards;

(2) your position relative to the button;

(3) your position relative to key players in the hand;

(4) your stack size;

(5) your stack size relative to the other players in the hand;

(6) the number of players in the hand;

(7) the number of players at the table;

(8) the quality of the players in the hand;

(9) whether or not the pot has been raised; and

(10) your table image.

Many of these criteria are interrelated with and/or dependent on one another, so you won't necessarily have to consider each of them in all situations. Let's take a brief look at each in turn.

Your cards: Clearly the quality of your cards is the simplest value to understand. Because the value of your cards is the easiest to interpret, many players stop there, but the card value is merely one small part of the overall picture. If you are old enough to remember the Cold War, then you'll recall that it wasn't about using the weapons but about having them. The word *deterrent* was tossed about quite a bit. If they thought we had weapons and believed we would use them, well, then, we didn't even need them. It's

---

[4] *This is based on live game play; in tournaments, there are other factors that come into play.*

often the same way with the cards. If you have sufficient advantage in the other areas, then the threat becomes more powerful than the execution.

Your position relative to the button: Position is extraordinarily valuable — much more so than the majority of your opponents understand. Therein lies its power. While even the most amateur rookie at your table understands that AA is powerful, even many experienced players don't play position correctly.

Your position relative to key players in the hand: Usually the idea of a key player in a hand refers to an aggressive player, whether he is a maniac or an excellent player. In LLNL, however, if you have a large stack, then the other large stacks are also key players.

Your stack size: You can enjoy a strategic advantage regardless of whether or not you have a large stack or a short stack. Your advantage, however, comes in different forms and impacts which hands you play and how you play them.[5]

Your stack size relative to the other players in the hand: I will often enter a pot with substandard cards against a player with $2,000 in front of him if I too have $2,000. It may cost me $5 to enter, but the possibility of 400:1 implied odds makes a lot of otherwise marginally or even unplayable hands become playable.

The number of players in the hand: Certain hands play well against many opponents but poorly against a small field. Conversely, some hands play well against one or two opponents but play poorly against a large field.[6]

---

[5] *See the sections "Playing a Big Stack" and "Playing a Short-Stack."*
[6] *See Appendices B and C.*

The number of players at the table: A short-handed table plays much differently than a full game. If there are only five people at the table, hand values change dramatically.[7]

The quality of the players in the hand: The quality of the players is often an overlooked issue. There is merit in playing an 86 against AA if the player with AA isn't able to get away from his hand if you hit big. On the other hand, if you are against a very good player who won't give you action if you do hit, then you'll do well not to become involved in the hand to begin with.

Whether or not the pot has been raised: If the pot has been raised, then you are getting significantly lower pot odds if you choose to continue. The more a pot has been raised, the more of an impact this criterion will have. Furthermore, in most cases, it means that you are up against a superior hand. This must impact your decision to continue.

Your table image: Your table image is what the other players think of you. If you haven't lost a pot all day and your table has noticed that, then you can certainly come in with hands that you may not have on another day. Conversely, if you've been getting beat all day, then your opponents may consider you ripe pickings, and therefore you must have the cards.

Let me set a scene. You are two off the button in a $2/$5 blind game. You've been getting beat like a drum all day, and the other players have noticed. Doyle Brunson is under-the-gun and raises to $20. To your left is Daniel Negreanu, who has been playing super-aggressively for the past hour. Six or seven players are seeing the flop every hand in this game. You have a below-average stack, and

---

[7] *See Appendices B and C.*

you look down and see two black aces. What do you do?

Did anyone say fold? I hope not. If you review our list, besides the value of your cards, apparently you have no other criterion that adds value to the strength of your hands, yet you will still play them — and you should. The point of this seemingly pointless question is that, if you can continue to play a hand that has just one value criterion working for it, you may begin to realize that often you have so much value added to your hand due to other criteria that the value of your cards no longer matters. This is, in fact, the case.

The following are three examples of recent hands I played when, due to other factors, the value of my cards didn't matter.

1. There is a young man I play with regularly who has read quite a few of the popular poker books and is very interested in improving his game. The problem is there aren't many books written on no-limit, and none has been written about LLNL. So where has he gotten most of his information from? From limit hold'em books. He has spent a great deal of time studying and learning what constitutes "good cards" pre-flop, and although he has been playing only a few months he is showing a great deal of talent already.

He is in EP and raises to $25, and the field folds to me on the button. What does he have? He has exactly what the book told him he is supposed to have: AA–JJ, AKs–AJs, AK–AQ.[8] He has $500 in front of him, and I have him

---

[8] While most limit books allow for such a range, the new no-limit player will usually tighten up even more significantly because the raise is more significant than in a limit game. During the play of the actual hand as well as previous experience with this particular player, I put him on AA–KK and perhaps AKs or QQ.

covered. I call with my 64o. If I can't beat one pair after the flop, I'm going to throw away. If I can, I'm going to bust him. 64o has better than one chance in six of outrunning AA. If, for a $25 investment, I can determine whether this is that one time, then I'm going to do it every time. I'll lose $25 five times for a total loss of $125 and win $500 once.

In this case, the quality of my opponent's play, my position relative both to the button and to my opponent, our respective stack sizes, my table image, and the number of players in the hand were the overwhelming features of the hand and the determining factors governing whether or not to come in.

2. There is a young woman I play with regularly who is frightened to death of getting involved in a pot with me. When she raises pre-flop and I can get her heads up, I simply call. If she doesn't flop the nuts, she's afraid to bet. If she bets, I almost certainly fold. If she checks, I bet, and she almost always folds — more than 90% of the time.

Let's look at the math in this case: let's say she raises pre-flop to $25. I call with two cards. I don't know or care what they are. There is $50 in the pot. If she bets post-flop, which occurs less than 10% of the time, I fold on those occasions that I haven't flopped a monster myself. Let's say she actually bets 10% of the time. That's too high, but let's give her the benefit of the doubt. Let's also say that I don't ever flop a big hand. Also not true, but I'll pad her numbers a bit. On the flop, she bets $50, 10 times out of 100, and I fold, losing my $25 pre-flop call 10 times for a total of $250. Ninety times out of 100 she checks, and I bet the pot ($50). She calls 10% of the time. Now I have $75 invested in this pot, and it might be time to look at my cards to see if I should bet the turn, because she will check it to me again. Since she called, it is very likely that she has the best hand, and let's say for the sake of argument that she always has the best hand if she calls me and that I will not bet again and never win in a showdown. Clearly that isn't possible, but again I'll pad her numbers. Nine times out of 100, I will lose $75 for a loss of $675, bringing my total losses to $925. Eighty-one times she folds when I bet the flop, thereby netting me her $25 pre-flop raise 81% of the time for a gain of $2,025. My net for the 100 hands, then, is $1,100 or $11 per hand. The pre-flop call, when the hand is played this way, has a positive expectation of $11 per occurrence or simply a positive EV of $11.

The number of players in the hand and my table image were the two key criteria that impacted the value of my hand. This woman is actually normally a very good player, but she considers me the luckiest person in the world, so her image of me negates the quality of her play when she is involved in a hand with me.

3. A very nice older gentleman was visiting Vegas from Florida and got into my game. He played very straight-forward. In other words, he bet when he had a hand and checked when he didn't. There was no deception in his play whatsoever, which is very dangerous in any no-limit game. He raised before the flop, and the rest of the field, having noted that he was playing tightly, mucked. I called. The flop came all rags, and he checked to me. I put him on a couple of big cards, most likely AK or AQ based on the raise and subsequent check. I'd called his initial raise before the flop with the intention of either hitting my hand or stealing the pot from him if we both missed. Although he had started with $100, he had only $80 left to call. Often inexperienced players will call with nothing,

hoping to become lucky on subsequent streets. If indeed he was one of these players, then I didn't want to push him in at this point, because with two cards to come he might feel like gambling. Instead, I waited for the turn, where, after a blank fell and he checked again, I pushed in. He raised before the flop and then checked both the flop and the turn. There was no chance that he had a piece of this board. None. I simply bet and won the pot. Again, the quality of my cards became a nonissue based on the quality of my opponent's play, the size of his stack, and my position in the hand relative to my opponent.

You'll note that I've given you no guidelines whatsoever in choosing which cards to come in with yet. That is a more appropriate way to begin a no-limit section on pre-flop standards than most players understand. It truly does "depend."

Playing Big Pairs Pre-Flop

In early position pre-flop with a big pair (AA, KK), I never raise on the strength of my pair. Yes, you read that right. That's not to say that I never raise while holding a big pair in early position, just that if I do raise it's for another reason. That reason might be that I have excellent control of the table or that I just won a couple of hands in a row with unlikely holdings that would increase the chance of getting more action than I would normally have coming, or some other such reason, but never simply on the strength of the pair. If I'm raised, then this is a different story altogether. This is what I'm hoping for. Then I'll often happily reraise and try to either win it right there or get my opponent to commit all his chips. If I simply get a call, then I'm going to bet the flop almost regardless of what comes.

This is, by the way, a very unpopular position. Players coming to low-limit no-limit from limit hold'em are scandalized by the thought. "You must protect your hand!" they cry. In limit, they are correct. Because of the huge implied odds in no-limit, however, deception is much more important than in limit. It's worth significantly more to maintain deception than it is to pick up an extra $5–$15 from a caller pre-flop.

In middle position with a big pair, when I am the first one in, I will typically limp if I feel there's a fair chance (30% or better) that I will be raised — if, for instance, there are some aggressive players in the game behind me. When I feel there's little chance of being raised, I will usually put in a standard raise for the table. If I'm not the first one in, then I'll almost always raise, usually trying to shut out everyone except the original bettor. Typically, when there is one early position limper for $5, I'll raise to about

$40, which is about two times the size of the pot. An amateur who limps in early position has a hand that he will have difficulty throwing away for $35 more, particularly against a player like me who has a reputation for splashing around. Therefore, I often get the hand heads up with position. When there is more than one limper, I will raise as well. The looser the game, the more I'll raise; I don't want a field coming with me. I'll risk the potential of a big hand and pick up the $15–$20 rather than take a big pair against the field. Usually, though, I'm raising so often that there's one brave, unbelieving soul who will try to keep me honest.

In late position, if I'm the first player in, I will usually make a $10–$15 raise. I'm hoping that it appears to be a steal raise and that one of the blinds will pop me back so I can reraise. If I'm in late position and there are callers, then I'm coming over the top; typically I'm going to raise about two times the size of the pot. If in late position I'm facing a raise, then I'm going to raise whatever amount I think it will take to isolate the original raiser.

While I usually suggest betting or raising about the size of the pot, I have recommended in a couple of situations here to raise about twice the size of the pot. There are a couple of reasons for doing this. First, and most obvious, I want to ensure that I shut out as many players behind me as possible and isolate a single player. Once one inexperienced player has come in, they all seem to fall into the pot like dominoes. Second, while a standard raise for the table may not get respect in the form of a fold, most inexperienced players tend to believe it means something about the quality of your hand. An oversized raise tends to indicate in the inexperienced player's mind that you are bluffing, and you will likely get that original caller to call the raise as a result.

Playing Other Pairs

Typically I am going to limp in and see a flop with any pair. As with the big pairs, I'm never going to raise solely on the strength of my hand, though I may raise for other reasons. When there are other reasons to raise, the larger my pair is, the more weight I will give it in the decision-making process. Limiting the field with hands such as QQ or JJ is not of such paramount importance as it is in limit games because before you can make any real money with these hands you are looking to flop a set. There is approximately an 8.6% chance in a 10-handed game that someone is holding AA or KK when you have QQ, almost a 13% chance that someone has a higher pocket pair when you are holding JJ. These numbers are uncomfortably high when your entire stack is at risk, as it is in LLNL. Further-more, if your raise is sufficient to get most hands out pre-flop, then the only hands likely to call you are AA, KK, and AK. You are a huge dog against either of the big pairs and merely a 6:5 favorite against AK, clearly not an enviable situation. Certainly the bigger the pair, the greater your likelihood of winning the pot, but while I'm usually aggressive with QQ and JJ in a limit game I slow way down in LLNL and treat them nearly as I would any other pair. I will limp with pairs other than AA or KK almost always, except perhaps in late position if I'm the first one in and the blinds are very tight. From the blinds too, I will usually limp and see a flop first even with QQ or JJ. I'm very aggressive at the table, and most players get the idea that I'm pushing them around, usually because I am. Turning over a JJ that I didn't raise with pre-flop when I'm in the blinds will usually slow down an opponent's attempt to play back at me for a few hours.

Another reason for just limping in with a pair is that I want a big field. TT, for instance, has almost a 30% chance of winning in a showdown six-handed, but if I am heads up it's usually against a coin flip at best. With two random cards, your equity in a six-handed pot is 16.67%, and your equity heads up is 50%. It's a much more desirable situation to have 30% equity in a pot you put 16.67% of the money into than to have 50% equity in a pot you had to put 50% of the money into.

Playing AK and AKs Pre-Flop

Although AKs is certainly a stronger hand than AKo, I usually play them the same pre-flop. As with big pairs and other premium hands, I limp with these hands in early position unless other factors indicate that a raise is correct. In contrast, I'd raise with AK strictly on the value of my cards in either a limit game or a traditional no-limit game. The mitigating circumstances that indicate a limp in LLNL are twofold.

> 1. First is the value of deception based on the quality of your opponents and their attentiveness. Most of the players whom you'll be playing against can't fathom a limp with **AK**, and they won't pay enough attention from one hand to another to observe that you rarely raise with it. Certainly, if you are playing against observant players, then you'll want to mix up your play somewhat, but most of the time observant opponents won't be an issue.
>
> 2. Second is the short stacks that one normally runs into in a LLNL game. For instance, if you are playing $1/$2 blind NL, you may find yourself facing an opponent who has just sat down with as little as $40. By raising pre-flop against stacks this small, you don't allow yourself the opportunity to outplay opponents after the flop.

While it's true that not raising allows hands to come in that will beat you on the flop, when you miss with AK, it's relatively easy to get away from the hand. If you get any action on the flop and have missed, then simply muck, and you will be out very little. The value of this hand in LLNL is when you hit and are able to collect off a hand that you have dominated. Most of the players whom you'll find yourself against in an LLNL game will pay you off when you have them outkicked.

The Suited Connectors

The suited connectors are a favorite of skilled no-limit players, and that includes LLNL. These are the types of hands that will bust an opponent quite easily and more often than other hands; you will have your opponents drawing dead when the money goes in. Although any two connecting cards of the same suit are of course suited connectors, when I speak of suited connectors I'm referring to a 54s and higher. The difference between a 32s and a 54s is significant in that you can only make two straights with a 32s and can make four straights with a 54s. Typically I call with suited connectors rather than raise, though I am capable of putting in a raise particularly in late position if I have good control of the table.

Consider this scenario: you're playing a $2/$5 blind NL game. You are on the button with 7♦6♦. There are five callers when the action gets to you, and including blinds there is $32 in the pot. You make it $40. Quite often in this spot I get no callers, one caller, two callers, or the whole field. Seldom do I get three or four callers, but that is great. I want everyone or no one. Suited connectors play very well against a large field. Clearly, when everyone throws away, I win $32. When everyone calls, I actually have a positive expectation against five or six random hands, and while their hands are probably not random — after all, they did voluntarily enter the pot for $5 and voluntarily call a raise — there is a good chance that many of the hands are in each other's way. So we're left with those situations when I get one or two callers. I have two advantages. Once again I have deception working for me; I raised to $40, so "obviously" I have better than a 7-high, right? Also, I have position. The deception works very well in this case because I have two ways to hit my hand. I can flop hard, in which case I'll have the best hand, or I can represent a big hand. If it's checked to me, I will make a pot-sized bet, say $100-$120. Watch your opponent. He will give you clues about whether or not he likes his hand. If he struggles to call, then a $300 bet on the turn will almost certainly finish him off. Note that it doesn't matter what the flop is. If he shows weakness, then stay on it.

Let's say you get a flop of AA2. Even if I was called pre-flop by a hand as good as A♠T♠, how can they call for all their chips?[9] They have to figure me for a bigger kicker if I turn the heat up. Now it's true that many bad players won't lay such a hand down, but they almost always will bet it at you on the flop to alert you to what they have. Nice of them, isn't it? If you get an unfavorable flop and you are bet into, then simply lay the hand down.

Let's say you get a great flop. Well, again, simply bet the hand out. I will usually drop my bet down a bit against unsuspecting players, however. Perhaps $75–$100 instead of the $100–$120 I recommended earlier. Checking to let them get something isn't the answer. They expect you to be aggressive. Even if they don't consciously realize what's going on, they will be wary of a check from the guy who's been pounding on them all day.

---

[9] *This is not to say that you go all-in on the flop, but if you are playing an aggressive style of poker a bet on the flop is almost always followed by a bet on the turn, and most players will figure that out pretty quickly against you.*

Trouble Hands

In a big no-limit game, hands that are overvalued and normally trouble are hands such as AQ, AJ, KQ, and KJ. In LLNL, if you hold AQ or AJ and are not raised, then you are very likely holding the best ace. The same principle holds true for KQ and KJ; you are probably holding the best king.

Because your opponents are likely to overvalue inferior hands and undervalue the worth of deception, trouble hands in LLNL are a bit different than you find in a regular no-limit game. Since your opponents tend not to be concerned about deception, they will usually be raising with those hands that can beat a traditional trouble hand. For instance, if you are holding a KQ, limp in, and aren't raised, then you can be confident that no one but the trickiest of your opponents has AQ or AK. With flops such as K♦7♥3♣ or Q♥8♣4♦, you should play the hand as if you are holding AK or AQ. In a big no-limit game, you must be very concerned about someone who limped with AK or AQ, but in this type of game you can almost be certain, if the pot wasn't raised pre-flop, that your king or queen is good if you are up against one pair.

AJo, another traditional trouble hand, is also a hand with which you can show more strength in LLNL when the pot hasn't been raised pre-flop. You are commonly going to find yourself involved with players in an LLNL game who will call a raise to come in with A9s or KTo, so they will certainly limp with it. Because your opponents are likely not only to come in with inferior holdings but also to pay you off when they hit, you must not, though still playing cautiously, become so tight that you throw these hands away without further information.

To illustrate my point, I recently found myself in middle position with AQo and was facing a $20 raise from the UTG player, who was a typical player. I called the raise, which I wouldn't have done in a big game, and the flop came A♦2♥3♠. He bet $40, and I raised to $100. After a period of thought, he decided to call, and I was convinced that I had him beat; if he had the straight, set, two pair, or even AK, I would have faced a reraise. I was clearly looking at an AT or AJ. As it turned out, he had an AJ, and I doubled through him. If this had been a big game, I would have either received no action or gone busted with an AQ if I had insisted on playing it. No player worth his salt would have raised under-the-gun with an AJ and then given me that much action after an ace fell.

Because your opponents have trouble overvaluing their hands, you can limp in with hands that you would, in a bigger game, pass. For instance, in late middle position, when there are callers but no raisers, I will often call with a hand such as A9 simply because it figures to be the best hand out there at that point. Although an ATs or an AJ doesn't warrant a raise based on card strength in early or middle position,[10] most of your opponents will be unaware of this and come in raising anyway. Since they haven't raised, I go ahead and limp along, hoping to hit an ace, which figures to be good if I do.

---

[10] *Such a hand may warrant a raise due to other factors, however.*

Size Counts

There are two issues to consider with regard to stack size: your stack size, and your opponent's stack size. If you have a large stack in relation to the max buy-in, then you generally want to play small pots whenever possible, unless, of course, you have a huge hand. Another consideration is the size of your stack relative to the size of your opponent's stack. If, for instance, I limp in late position with A♠K♠, the flop brings an A♦6♣4♥, and a typical opponent in middle position bets $20, then my responses would be different, depending on the relationship between our respective stacks.

The examples that follow are meant to provide a general template with which to give you an idea of how I might play against a typical opponent. Since the term "typical" is somewhat vague, look for general principles, not precision, as *your* "typical" opponent may be different from *mine.*

There is $20 in the pot, and my opponent bets $20 on the flop.

If I have $600 in front of me and he has me covered: In this case, I would simply call. My opponent is going to be concerned about the damage that I can do to his chip stack in most cases. Also, if he has been at the table long enough to amass more chips than me, and I've been able to build to $600, then he likely knows that I play deceptively. The call in this spot is both cautious and an attack of sorts. He has to be concerned that I'm setting a trap, so his action on the turn will tell me a lot about the strength of his hand.

If I have $600 and he has $300: In this spot, I raise to

$80. Here I am basically telling him that it's going to cost him the rest of his chips on the turn. My hand figures to be the best at that moment, but I'd just as soon find out now. If he raises me all-in, then I will likely throw away barring any further information.

If I have $600 and he has $100: I will put him all-in. I'll take the pot right now if he'll let me have it, but for $100 we might as well get it all-in now. It makes no sense to raise to $80, as in the previous example, and face a $20 all-in bet from him on the turn. I certainly won't throw away a $200 pot in this spot for a $20 all-in bet,[11] so I'll waste no time and push in, giving him an opportunity to muck. Incidentally I consider it unlikely that the typical LLNL player will muck in this spot. I have to figure him for an ace.[12] If he is making a move without an ace, then he's not going to be putting any money into the pot on the turn anyway.

If I have $100 and he has $100 or more: Again, I will push all-in. I am not afraid to go broke; I will simply buy more chips, but he may well want to hang on to some money. Some of your opponents may be willing to throw the best hand away in this spot for all their chips.[13]

Let's look at those times when my opponent checks on the flop.

If I have $600 in front of me and he has me covered: I will bet $20 here. I'll take the pot right now if he'll let me have

---

[11] *This is based, of course, on the ambiguity of his holdings.*
[12] *Of course, he may have two pair or a set, but this doesn't change my play.*
[13] *In this particular case, it would be very unlikely that an opponent would throw away a hand that could beat AK, with the possible exception of 64, but in many cases your opponent will have a much larger range of winning hands he is willing to muck.*

it, but I have a strong enough hand to take a little heat. If he check-raises me, then I'll have to take my opponent into consideration, but in most cases I will call a pot-sized bet and invite him to bet the turn. If he checks the turn, he is usually facing another bet.

If I have $600 and he has $300: Again I will bet $20. If he check-raises me here, then I will usually push all-in.

If I have $600 and he has $100: I will bet the pot. If he check-raises, it will likely be all-in, and I will call most opponents.

If I have $100 and he has $100 or more: I will bet $30, preparing for all-in on the turn.

Chapter 6

Post-Flop: Who Is More Likely to Go Broke?

Who, as a result of this action, is more likely to go broke, me or my opponent? This question is the cornerstone of successful LLNL play. If you can make break-even decisions but filter each of those decisions through this one question, then you'll be well on your way to success. This isn't about how to value-bet to squeeze an extra $10 out of your opponent. That's not the point of no-limit. You may of course find yourself in a situation in which a value bet is correct, but it, like everything else in no-limit, is secondary to your primary task: busting or doubling through your opponent. Let's take a look at how this applies to no-limit pre-flop standards.

For the sake of these examples, let's assume that you just sat down in a new $2/$5 no-limit game and have never played with any of the players before. Every player starts with $300; you have drawn seat four with the button in seat one; you're UTG. Which hands do you want to come in with? The answer is precious few right now because you know very little about your opponents and have the worst position.

Let's say you're dealt KK your first hand. What do you do? Fold? Who, as a result of this action, is more likely to go broke, you or your opponent? Well, actually you are. If you start throwing away KK pre-flop for a single bet, you're not going to last long. Therefore, folding is incorrect.

Call? Who, as a result of this action, is more likely to go broke, you or your opponent? If you call, you allow your opponents to come in cheaply, almost certainly with inferior hands. On the other hand, by simply calling, you maintain deception about the strength of your hand. You're faced with a decision.

Raise? Who, as a result of this action, is more likely to go broke, you or your opponent? Let's assume that, if you are going to raise, you will make a standard pre-flop raise, perhaps the size of the pot. You may drive out some inferior hands, but you will lose the value of deception. Your opponents will know that you have a premium hand. Again, you are faced with a decision.

Clearly the question comes down to raising or calling. The answer, like all good poker answers, is "It depends."

The 12 Mistakes

In what I hold to be one of the most profound poker essays of all time, David Sklansky wrote about the "eight mistakes in poker." My chapter here is adapted from the concepts he introduced in that excellent essay. Sklansky listed eight instead of 12 because he was writing for a limit audience; however, since this book refers to LLNL, I will address 12 mistakes. While these mistakes can be made throughout the play of a hand and during any round of betting, we will address them from a post-flop perspective. In any form of big bet poker, pre-flop errors that would be critical in limit are usually relatively insignificant and can almost always be overcome by expert play post-flop. By examining each of the mistakes, you can achieve two goals: the reduction of mistakes in your game, and the ability to induce these errors in your opponents.

1. Checking When You Should Bet

The most common example of this mistake is checking a powerful hand in the hope of eliciting a bet so that one can check-raise.[1] This mistake, while the most common, is not the most costly.

A second example is having betting standards that are too high when you have a strong hand. For instance, if you held A♦A♥, and had bet a flop of A♣9♥5♦ but failed to bet the turn when an 8♠ fell, out of fear of a straight, then your betting standards were certainly too high. While this example is extreme, lesser cases would also qualify as mistakes.

---

[1] *There is more on the lack of wisdom associated with that move in the section on check-raising.*

And a third example is failing to bet when both you and your opponent hold a weak hand, your opponent is likely winning, yet he can't call if you bet. This aspect of the mistake is probably the most costly one routinely made. Whenever you bet, there are two ways for you to win. You might win because you have the best hand, or you might win because you cause your opponent to throw away an equal or better hand. If it's unlikely that you will win the hand in a showdown, it's often correct to bet if that bet will cause your opponent to throw away even occasionally. If there is $300 in the pot and your opponent will fold to a $200 bet even half the time, then you should certainly bet. You will lose $200 once and win $300 once for a net win of $100.[2]

2. Betting When You Should Check
The most common form of this error is when a player bets a hand that will be called by a hand that can beat him, but not by a hand that he can beat. An example might be a player who is holding the Q♠Q♦, and the board shows a Q♣J♦A♠2♦T♠. Betting on the river will only elicit a call from a player with the straight. An opponent with two pair will not call you regardless, so you should check. Especially if you are prepared to call a bet from an opponent who is prone to bluffing, you should check and allow him the opportunity to bluff.

An important general poker principle to keep in mind when we explore this mistake is that it takes a stronger hand to call a bet than it does to bet. If you have a very strong

---

[2] *The net win of $100 is for two such occurrences; your EV on such a play is $50.*

hand that can either bet or call a bet, but you suspect that your aggressive opponent behind you has a hand that is only strong enough to bet, then you should check it to him. Since he won't call your bet anyway, your only chance to make more money is to get him to do the betting.

This is particularly important when the pot is multiway and the opponent you are checking to is loose as well as aggressive. Because of his loose-aggressive tendencies, he may get calls that you would not. Often a bet from you will fold the field, but a bet from the resident maniac will cause another player or two to call with weak holdings. In this case, a bet from you may lose multiple bets.

3. Betting Insufficiently When Betting Is Correct
This mistake isn't possible in fixed-limit poker, though it can happen in both big bet poker and spread limit poker. A common situation arises when a player attempts a bluff with a bet that is so small in relation to the size of the pot that it makes it overwhelmingly correct for her opponent to call. If, for instance, she bet $10 when a scare card fell on the river but the pot was $140, then her opponent would be correct to call if there was just one chance in 15 that she was bluffing.

Another situation, particularly common in LLNL, is when a player bets a strong hand but ensures that her opponent has sufficient odds to call. For instance, an early position player raises to $10 pre-flop with Q♠Q♥ in a $1/$2 blind game and gets five callers. The pot is $60, the flop comes 9♦8♣2♦, and she bets $10 into the field. The first player to act is getting 7:1 on a call and may be correct to call with as little as AK and certainly with a diamond flush draw or open-ended straight draw. Often I listen to bad beat stories from players who make this error. They have been drawn out on, yet they have ensured that their opponents had the correct odds to do so on every betting round.

4. Betting Excessively When Betting Is Correct

This mistake, like the previous one, is common among inexperienced LLNL players. Often, when an inexperienced player finds himself in possession of the ever elusive nuts, he bets an amount that no one can hope to call. It's not unusual to see such a player go all-in for $100 or even more into a pot that barely has $10 in it.

One doesn't need the nuts for a large bet to be a mistake; if your opponent is willing but incorrect to call a $20 bet but won't call a larger bet, then you should bet $20.[3] For instance, if you hold the 7♦7♠ and the flop comes A♥7♣2♠, then you would have a very strong hand and may make a great deal of money off an unsuspecting player with a big ace. A pot-sized bet is usually called for in such a case and will almost certainly be called or even raised, but an all-in bet would likely chase your opponent out of the pot when he is drawing very slim.

5. Folding When You Should Call

This mistake is most likely to be made by a player who plays too tightly. This can be either a tight-aggressive player or a tight-passive player. The tight-aggressive player who is prone to this mistake is much more likely to make

---

[3] *This amount is predicated on the assumption that your bankroll isn't in jeopardy. If it is, then you are playing too high for your bankroll and should step down in limits.*

this error in a limit game, where the size of the bet is much smaller in relation to the size of the pot, than he is in a big bet game. For instance, let's say he is playing in a $15/$30 limit game, is holding the A♠T♠, and the board shows a K♠T♥2♠2♥7♦. Let's say he fails to complete his flush draw, so he folds to a $30 bet into a $300 pot on the river. If, for instance, there was a one-in-seven chance that his opponent was on a busted draw of his own and bluffing, then this would be a mistake. If, however, the game is no-limit, he is less likely to make an error simply because the size of the final bet may be too large for a call to be correct. If, on the river, he finds himself facing a $300 bet, as might well be the case in a no-limit game, then folding would almost certainly be correct. For this reason, the structure often protects tight-aggressive players from making this error.

The tight-passive players, on the other hand, are lining up to make this mistake in LLNL. While they are certainly capable of making the error that I discussed above, they are much less likely to make it only because they are so less frequently in contention for the pot by the river. When these players make this error, they tend to make it on the earlier rounds, on the flop or less frequently on the turn. While the tight-aggressive player tends to make his error based on out-thinking himself and trying to save a bet, these players tend to make this error by ignoring implied odds and seeing only the decimation of their stack in the near future.

6. Folding When You Should Raise

As with the previous mistake, this error is most likely to be made by a player who plays too tightly. While not as common as the previous mistake, it too is usually made by tight-passive players. Tight-aggressive players choosing between two close choices, to either raise or fold, tend to err in the raising department. Even though this is an error made often by tight players, it rarely tends to affect tight-aggressive players in LLNL.

Folding when one should raise occurs when the player is holding a strong hand and misinterprets the strength of her hand or when she is holding a weak or mediocre hand and fails to account for the weakness in her opponent's hand. In both instances, it's a case of misinterpreting the relative value of one's hand.

The first case, misinterpreting the strength of one's hand when one is holding a strong hand, unless someone has mis-read the hand, often happens when one is on a draw. For instance, if a player is holding the J♥T♥, and the flop brings a 9♥8♥2♣, then she is holding a very strong hand. The strength is based on the drawing potential of the hand, with two cards to come. While simply calling may be the correct play with such a hand, many times such a hand would call for a raise. A player who would fold such a hand, while rare, would be very tight indeed. Against a player willing to make a fold such as this, you should be much more aggressive with her in order to induce such a mistake.

The second case, when a player is holding a weak or mediocre hand and fails to account for the weakness in her opponent's hand, most often occurs when a tight player is being bluffed. For instance, it often happens that, if there's little interest in the board and it's been checked down, a more aggressive player may bet in an effort to get her tight opponent to lay down a hand that the aggressive player is unsure she can beat in a showdown. If the tight player is also holding a weak hand, then she may fold when a raise would almost surely win her the pot.

7. Calling When You Should Fold

This mistake is most commonly made by players who are playing too loosely: typically loose-passive players and less frequently loose-aggressive players. This is the most common mistake in LLNL. This application of the error isn't complicated to understand; if a player should fold, then he must have insufficient chances to win the pot. He may have insufficient pot odds to make calling correct, or worse he may be drawing dead. It's easy to induce this mistake from your calling station-type opponents; just bet when you have the best hand. While that may sound too obvious to mention, it fails to happen these days with alarming regularity. We seem to have entered the "Age of Playing Reverse Poker," in which players, in an effort to be sneaky, bet when they don't have the best hand in an effort to bluff and check when they have a hand in an effort to check-raise. One can make a case for the occasional use of these types of plays, but not against a player who calls when he should fold. Against these players, you must bet to induce their mistakes.

Another situation in which players routinely make this mistake is when they call on a draw, believing they are getting sufficient implied odds, but fail to consider whether they will be called if they make their hands. For instance, many a player who finds himself with a hand such as A♠J♦ will call a pot-sized bet on a board of Q♠9♠7♣2♠, thinking that, because he is drawing to the nut spade flush, he should call. It is the rare opponent who would pay him off if he made his flush with four spades on board. In this case, his implied odds aren't as good as they appear to be, and a pot-sized bet is simply too much to call against most opponents.

8. Calling When You Should Raise

Calling, as we've discussed, is frequently the worst choice a player can make, yet it's the one most players choose. There are three reasons why people choose to call when it would be correct to raise. Let's start by defining "correct": I mean that your expectation increases by raising instead of calling.

The first reason that people make this mistake is because they are trying to slow-play. In LLNL, because of the large implied odds, it's often correct to try to win the pot immediately. By raising, there are necessarily less implied odds available because your stack is smaller after a raise. When this error is made in LLNL, it frequently costs you your entire stack. This mistake, when made for this reason, tends to be made by aggressive players getting too tricky for their own good.

The next instance when a player makes this mistake is when he doesn't know where he is in the hand. If, for instance, his opponent turned over his hand and showed it to him, then he would raise instead of just calling. This error is based on a lack of awareness usually brought about by a passive style. While a passive style refers to a playing style, it is usually reflective of a person's personality too. Putting someone on a hand takes effort and experience; these players tend to be playing for fun, so it's not worth the effort. This version of the mistake is usually made by LPPs.

Another situation is when a player is playing scared, which is the domain of the TPP. Unlike the previous instance, if his opponent turned over his cards and showed the TPP what he had, then the TPP would still probably not raise. He would wait for a lock on the river to raise.

Unlike the other mistakes, this one is difficult to induce unless you too make an error. If you bet while your opponent has a raising hand that he won't fold, then you are incorrect to bet and therefore can't induce the error without making one of your own. You can, however, still take advantage of a player's predisposition to make this mistake. If you are in a multiway pot and have a player behind you who often makes this mistake, then you might be more willing to call when you are on a draw, knowing that he is more likely just to call.

9. Raising When You Should Fold

The type of player most likely to make this mistake is the aggressive player, both loose and tight. Although either type can make this error, it's more often a mistake made by tight-aggressive players, who understand that raising is often a close, but more preferable, option to folding. If the decision is close, then an error can easily be made. Unfortunately this type of player makes fewer errors than the other players you'll face, so you might easily misinterpret this error as a sign of strength. Again, however, if you have a strong hand, you should bet into your tight-aggressive opponents since they will be more likely to make this costly error than the other player types.

The loose-aggressive player will also make this mistake but with significantly greater results than he might in a limit game. In a tough game, he will still lose, but he won't lose nearly as much as he would in a typical limit game. As a result of the increasing sizes of the bets in LLNL, a raise when a fold would have been correct tends to be very large and will often cause an opponent behind him to make the mistake of folding when he should raise.[4] As with the TAP, you should be more aggressive with your strong hands against the LAP since he is more likely to make the error of raising. Too many players try for a check-raise when a straightforward bet works better.

10. Raising When You Should Call

Once again, the type of player to make such a mistake is an aggressive player, both loose and tight. A tight player, nursing his aversion to calling, often raises during those instances when a call is actually the best option. A good example is when he's on a draw and decides to raise to try to win the pot right there when he has little chance of doing so or to drive opponents out. In most cases, when you are on a drawing hand, you want people to stay in order to increase the odds you are getting from the pot. Loose-aggressive players who make this error are often trying to bluff their opponents when there is no chance that their opponents will fold and get value out of a call but get diminishing value out of a raise.

Another instance of this mistake is the player who raises when by doing so he shuts out callers (or reraisers) behind him and makes no further money by doing so. For instance, let's say that a player with a history of bluffing makes a large bet on the river when it completes a flush. You have the nut flush, and there's a player to act behind you. Since the player who made the bet is a known bluffer,

---

[4] *Certainly you could argue that if his raise caused his opponent to throw away then it was not a mistake. The situations I am referring to are those in which a raise will cause his opponent to throw away occasionally but not enough for the raiser to turn a profit.*

you may get a call from the player behind you, but only if you call. That player may believe that you too are calling based on the first player's history of bluffing and that it doesn't necessarily indicate a strong hand. But if you raise, he will realize that you do in fact have a hand and won't call. It's important to note here, if the original bettor was bluffing, then he isn't going to call your raise anyway, so you make no further money by raising.

11. Raising Insufficiently When Raising Is Correct

This mistake is common in LLNL. There has been a tendency in recent years to raise the minimum or, as it is frequently referred to, "min raise." While there are times when a min raise is a reasonable play, it's not always so. There are two common cases where it's a mistake.

In the first case, a player with a weak or drawing hand min raises to get a free card. This is a tactic borrowed from limit in an attempt to "buy a free card," but its downside can be significantly worse in no-limit. A min raise almost never wins the pot in a drawing situation, while a significant raise, against a weak player, may in fact do so. If you have almost no chance of winning the pot immediately, then you merely decrease the immediate odds you are getting for your draw and leave yourself open to a large reraise, which could force you out.

In the second case, a player is playing a strong hand and raises an amount that alerts an opponent to use caution yet earns the raiser the minimum. It's not uncommon, especially against weak opposition, for a large raise to be seen as a bluff attempt and a small raise as an indication of great strength by a player who is trying to be deceptive. If your opponent is likely to misinterpret a pot-sized or larger bet as a bluff attempt, then you should bet this larger amount.

12. Raising Excessively When Raising Is Correct

It is frequently correct to raise, yet in LLNL a player will often raise an amount that is incorrect. The most common occurrence of this mistake is when a player raises so much that an opponent who is prepared to make a lesser mistake now refrains and mucks. For instance, if you were holding the A♠Q♠, the flop brought a K♦J♠T♣, and your opponent bet $30 into the $30 pot, then a raise would usually be called for. Assuming that you both had $500 in front of you, a pot-sized raise of $90 may cause your opponent to call when he should be folding, but a $500 raise may cause him to fold, saving him both the immediate $90 and any further mistakes on future streets.

A second example of this mistake is when a player is bluffing when a bluff attempt is called for. Often there is nothing a pot-sized bet or even less won't accomplish that an overbet will. For instance, let's say that the flop brought a K♠T♦2♠ and you put your opponent on a draw but were uncertain if he was on a straight draw or a flush draw. If the pot had $100 in it and the turn brought a 6♠, you might try a bluff of $75, which he will almost certainly raise if he hits his flush and fold if he's on a straight draw. However, since he will certainly not be dissuaded from calling if he does hit his flush, a bet of $500 would be a mistake.

A final form of this mistake is when your raise is so large as to get players out behind you who would cold-call a lesser raise. While this is a rare form of this error, it also points to a practical use of the min raise concept.

Parlaying Decisions: When to Get the Money In

- Against a player who is much better than you, you want to get all your chips into the pot as quickly as possible.
- Against a player who is much worse than you, you want to get all your chips into the pot as slowly as possible.

Let's take a quick refresher course in statistics before we continue. If you flip a fair coin, since a coin has only two sides, the probability of flipping heads versus tails is one in two. If you flip the coin again, the probability of it coming up heads again is also one in two. Each coin flip is an independent event and as such is not affected by previous flips. What about the probability associated with coming up a winner on two or more consecutive rounds? Calculating the odds for multiple flips is simple and helpful in terms of understanding the probability of seeing strings of back-to-back events.

What is the probability of flipping two heads in a row? This is calculated by taking the one-in-two probability and multiplying it by itself, which turns out to be one in four. In this case, the combined probability of one in four means that in four consecutive two-flip sets only one of them will likely produce back-to-back heads. Since there are twice as many ways that two flips can turn out, the probability against success therefore becomes doubled. The two flips can yield a combination of heads-heads, heads-tails, tails-heads, or tails-tails, and only one of the four two-flip sets meets our requirements. Okay, enough of the refresher course and on to its application to poker.

Let's say that you are much better than your opponent. So much so in fact that, on average, you'll make a better decision than your opponent 70% of the time. This isn't at all far-fetched. I'd say that this situation occurs quite often in actual play against specific opponents. Keep in mind that you are reading this book trying to improve your game, while he's playing Nintendo while wearing sunglasses.

If, when you think you have the best hand pre-flop and have decided correctly that your opponent will call your all-in bet, you push in, then you will, in fact, have the best hand 70% of the time. Keep in mind our filter: who, as a result of this action, is more likely to go broke, me or my opponent? Well, clearly the answer is that your opponent is more likely to go broke. Seventy percent of the time you'll have the best hand, so your opponent will go broke more often. Let's say you decide that this is going to be your ongoing strategy. If you push all-in twice against this opponent, then you are actually an underdog to win both times. Your opponent has a 51% chance of going in with the best hand during at least one outcome, a 42% chance of being correct once, and a 9% chance of being correct twice. If your opponent is correct once, which he is a favorite to be, and the cards break even, then so will the chips. Is there a better course of action?

Keeping the same percentages in mind, let's refrain from pushing all-in before the flop. Your opponent makes it $25 to go, and you believe that you have the best hand right now, but you simply decide to call. Your opponent, of course, thinks that he has the best hand, but it's only 30% likely that he is correct. Now the flop comes, and your opponent bets $50. You consider the flop. After analysis, you decide that you still have the best hand and that your opponent has little chance of drawing out on you; therefore, just calling is the better decision. You have now made another decision in which you are likely to be correct 70% of the time, and more important you have forced your opponent to make a decision of whether or not to bet that (because you called) figures to be right only 30% of the time. Because you are causing this hand to become a series of decisions for your opponent, and because you have a huge edge in decision-making abilities, your opponent's likelihood of winning this hand is dropping. At this stage of the hand, he has been faced with two decisions, both of which he is an underdog to make correctly. In actuality, you are making him parlay 30% shots from betting round to betting round. After only two such decisions, he has only a 9% chance of having played the hand correctly to this point.

By just calling on the flop, he is faced with another decision whether to bet or to check on the turn. If he bets and you decide that a call is correct, then he has only a 30% chance that his turn bet will be correct, bringing him down to a 2.7% chance that he has played this hand correctly to this point. On the river, we will force him to make another decision. This decision, like all his others, has a 30% chance of being correct, which will make his chances of having played the hand correctly all the way through a paltry 0.81%. If he decides to check at any point in the hand, then we will simply bet, and he will be faced with a different decision in which he has the same likelihood of error. In no-limit, one error is usually enough. Give your opponents every opportunity to make one.

This isn't to say that you have a 99.19% chance of having made the right decisions all the way through. Actually you have a 99.19% chance of not having made all your decisions incorrectly. But compare this to our first example, when you went all-in before the flop and had only a 70% chance of not having made all your decisions incorrectly. By giving yourself only one decision, you've handicapped yourself. Conversely, your opponent in our previous example had a 30% chance of making all his decisions correctly, but in the second case he had only a 0.81% chance of doing so. He's over 37 times more likely to have made all his decisions correctly in the first case than in the second.

This also points to your optimal strategy against a player who is much better than you. Imagine for a moment that Doyle Brunson is sitting across from you and he raises the pot: if you believe you have the best hand and are planning on playing it, then your best course of action may very well be to go all-in now. In fact, this principle was demonstrated poignantly at the 2004 World Series of Poker as hundreds of new players, many of them never having played live poker before, began putting their professional opponents all-in at the drop of a hat, in some cases before the hat actually hit the floor. Many top professionals lost their composure while they desperately struggled to find a way to get the edge back that they were losing through this strategy.

When the Situation Is Close

- If you play better than your opponents, then when the situation is close there is always a better spot.

Recently Chris, a student and friend of mine who is an accomplished player, discussed an interesting hand that came up in a $2/$5 blind NL game. He had the T♣9♣ on the button and limped in behind three other players. The small blind folded, and the big blind, a remarkably tight-passive player, checked. The flop came 8♣7♣4♥, and the big blind immediately pushed all-in for the $500 he had in front of him. It was folded around to Chris with the T♣9♣. Because of the predictability of this tight-passive player, Chris knew that he could only have the straight. This player hadn't gone all-in without the nuts since Grant took Richmond.[5] Chris knew what most people at the table probably didn't know: namely, that his draw was powerful enough to be a favorite against the current nuts with two cards to come: 51% to 49%[6] for $500. Chris didn't call, and he was correct in not calling despite having an advantage.

It has been my experience that most players in an LLNL game wouldn't have called either, but for very different reasons. Most LLNL players whom you'll encounter would simply be afraid of the size of the bet when all they had was a draw. To his credit, this wasn't the reason Chris didn't call. He didn't call because this was a tight-passive, unimaginative player who was easy to beat. Chris had $800 in front

---

[5] *April 1865. Yeah, I had to look it up.*
[6] *Based on 14 outs. Since Chris knew that this player had the straight, he also knew that one of his outs, a six, wasn't available.*

of him and had the table covered in a max $300 buy-in game. This $800 gave him a lot of leverage against those players with shorter stacks, and that leverage was worth money. He knew that if he simply waited he'd be able to get this player's money when he had much more favorable odds without risking the extra equity he'd built up by increasing his chip stack. It is rarely correct[7] to take a close call in an LLNL game against a weak player, even one in which you have an advantage if, by doing so, you'll go busted or become a short stack again.

[7] See the following chapter for the exception.

Building a Stack

This may be the most controversial chapter in this book. Many traditional no-limit players won't be able to naturally adjust to this type of thinking and will resist it. Notwithstanding, it's a very powerful strategic technique. Before we explore this strategy, let's consider the following reality.

Low-limit no-limit has more in common with another common poker venue than it does with traditional no-limit. That venue is the re-buy tournament. As in the re-buy tournament, a player sitting down at a low-limit no-limit game has a predetermined limit to the number of chips he can buy. In a re-buy tournament, the amount of chips a player sits down with is fixed, while in an LLNL game the *maximum* amount of chips a player can sit down with is fixed. The significance of this slight difference is negligible. The second commonality that the LLNL structure shares with the re-buy tournament is that you can only re-buy once you've fallen below a predetermined minimum number of chips.[8]

So how does this change your strategy from a regular no-limit game? The chips in front of you when you first sit down are easily replaceable; you can risk them more easily in an effort to double or triple up, thereby gaining the leverage that a big stack gives you. Once you've built your stack to a healthy level of two or more times the maximum buy-in, it's time to protect those chips. In a game with $100 maximum buy-in, the first $100 costs you exactly $100, but additional chips aren't for sale at any price, and

---

[8] *Some re-buy tournaments allow you to re-buy immediately, before falling below a certain number of chips, but this is the exception.*

that makes them worth more to an expert player.[9] Why is that? Well, by way of example, let's take a look at the situation that Daniel Negreanu found himself in during the 2004 WSOP's seventh event, the $1,000 buy-in no-limit hold'em event with re-buys.

You may recall that this was the event that Negreanu re-bought an unprecedented 27 times, eventually capturing third place and a hefty $72,000 in profit. Twenty-seven re-buys? What was he thinking? Was the 2004 Player of the Year simply on tilt? There were more than 50 re-buys at this particular tournament table, which put over $60,000 in chips in play. Negreanu then switched gears and played his fierce brand of poker, gaining a good portion of the chips in play. At a level where top players on other tables were struggling through careful play to double up their $1,000 in starting chips, Negreanu had built a mountain of chips by dumping a truckload of chips on the table and then winning them back. In tournaments, having a large chip stack has always offered the expert player advantages, but due to the largely inexperienced fields you find today a large chip stack is even more advantageous. The reason lies in the fact that, for the most part, it's the inexperienced players who still remain at the halfway point of a tournament who have the largest chip stacks. Traditionally correct play doesn't include a lot of gambling in the early stages of a tournament. As a result, it's rare to find an expert player being among the chip leaders at the halfway mark. Instead, they have added modestly to their stacks and put themselves in a position to chip away at those inexperienced players

[9] *Actually this reference is in regard to live games with a max buy-in rather than a tournament.*

who have faded the odds and built a mountain of chips on poor play. The expert player who finds himself in possession of an equally large stack doesn't have to "chip away" at his less experienced opponent; he can take him down in a single hand, doubling up in the process.

The same strategy works in low-limit no-limit games. Now, while it's true that players in a live game can cash out whenever they want to, this is compensated by the fact that the re-buy period never ends, and the fish you've had your eye on for the past two hours won't be moved to another table.

When I first sit down to an LLNL game, I buy-in for the maximum. If there are many large stacks at the table, as is frequently the case when I arrive at a game already in progress, it behooves me to amass as many chips as possible as quickly as possible. As the best player, or one of the best players, in the game, I have a significant edge over the majority of players whom I'll sit down with. If I buy-in for the maximum, say $100, that's all I can win from an individual player in a single hand. Unfortunately I'm greedy. If I have $600 in front of me when the perfect opportunity comes up, which usually occurs a couple of times per session, I could win $600 in a single hand against a specific opponent (clearly I could win more if there was multiway action, but I'm discussing a heads-up situation that will be most common). Finding myself short-stacked when that hand comes up isn't a position I want to be in. Therefore, I will usually gamble when I first sit down in an effort to collect a healthy stack as quickly as possible. At first glance, this suggestion can look like a negative EV proposal, but there are two reasons why it isn't.

First, when I say that I'm willing to gamble, I am discussing situations in which I am not an overwhelming favorite, or even those in which I am even money, but usually not cases in which I am clearly getting insufficient odds. Second, when you figure in your long-term implied odds over a session or even multiple sessions, if you are playing against the same people, you can begin to see how this strategy can work. Most often implied odds are thought about in terms of future betting rounds within the same hand, but that idea is short-sighted and doesn't capture the whole picture.

By way of an extreme example, here is a hand that I played recently in which a willingness to gamble in order to build a chip stack had very positive consequences. I joined a $1/$2 blind no-limit game and sat down right behind the button with the maximum buy-in of $100. One player has accumulated $600, and the rest of the table seems to be equally split between players having about $300 and the other half sitting on about $100. The game's been pretty restrained up till now, but in the next hand the under-the-gun player opens for $20, and his raise is called in three spots before it gets to me. I look down to see the 8♣2♣; I call. The big blind raises to $100, and everyone, including me, calls. The pot is $600 pre-flop, and the player in the big blind moves all-in in the dark. Everyone not already all-in folds on the flop of 2♠2♥7♣, and he turns over his K♥K♦. He receives no improvement, and I pick up the pot.

I'll fill you in on my thinking. Mine was clearly a garbage hand, but I'd be getting 4:1 on a $20 call, position on the field, and a chance to double up even without implied odds, triple, or better if I hit. This wasn't the type of hand I'd lose any money on after the flop; I had to either hit it hard or be done with it, so at that point I was risking at most $20. I decided to call. The big blind raised to $100, and by the time it got back to me the pot was now offering me $520 for an $80 call or 6.5:1. If I called, then I would have lost any implied odds I'd hoped to gain because I'd be all-in. Now, I want to make it clear that, while calling with a garbage hand usually has a clear and overwhelmingly negative expectation, 8♣2♣ against five random hands is actually just about 6.5:1. While the probability is that I was up against much better than random hands with so many people willing to put $100 in pre-flop, the balancing feature is that many of those hands could be in each other's way, and that's exactly what happened. When I plugged the actual hands into Mike Caro's Poker Probe, I found that while I was 6.5:1 underdog against five random hands I was 5.8:1 against the actual hands.

Normally, of course, I don't want an even money situation or anything close. You'll recall that earlier I recommended passing close situations and waiting for those opportunities that present more significant advantages, especially when you play better than your opponents. Although the math was close, there were other factors that made this call more profitable than it might, at first glance, appear.

A single hand doesn't make a game. A few things are going to happen after this hand that will increase my equity, my long-range implied odds, if you will. I'm going to proudly turn over my 8♣2♣ regardless of whether or not I hit and will be labeled the "livest" one at the table. If I lose, there will be another $100 on the table that I can potentially win. If I win, I will have $600, I will be the "chip leader" at the table, and I will then revert to a much more selective style of play while being guaranteed almost unlimited action by those who watched me make such a "foolish" play. These added incentives increase my equity in the call enough to tip the balance.

This type of strategy isn't for everyone, and it requires a couple of caveats. You *must* be one of the best players at the table. I know what you are thinking: how good does one have to be to push $100 in with a garbage hand? You are right; you don't have to be good to do this. You do, however, have to be very good in order to capitalize on what you earn. You must have excellent hand-reading skills to know that your AK is good when you push your newly won $600 all-in down the line on a flop of AKQ. Contrary to appearances, you must have great self-control as well. Playing a garbage hand for all your chips when one is getting 6.5:1 doesn't take an enormous amount of self-control, but *not* playing it, when you're getting only 2 or 3:1 because you've already dumped $300 into the game and you're beginning to panic, does. You also have to know how to use a big stack to bully other players in order to make the most out of this strategy. If you aren't yet comfortable pushing people around, then the big stack probably isn't worth it, and you won't get fair value out of the risk you take to get there. Also, you must be able to change gears and put on the brakes hard. After a hand like this, you are much more likely to get callers; this is great if you have a hand, but forget about bluffing for a while.

This particular example is extreme. I chose it to illustrate how even a normally worthless hand under the right circumstances can be used profitably. Typically, however, when you are prepared to gamble in order to build a large stack quickly, you should still be more selective than this hand illustrates.

Small Bet Poker

Small bet poker is defined as making small bets in order to keep the pot small, holding off on making as much of an investment as you can until you have an overwhelmingly large advantage. Small bet poker is primarily a tournament concept; however, as I've discussed previously, LLNL has some strong similarities to the re-buy tournament, and as a result small bet poker has more value in LLNL than in most other cash games. Playing small bet poker has two distinct advantages.

The first advantage is that it often increases your expectation. Consider the following example. I was playing in a $2/$5 blind no-limit game and had run my initial $500 buy-in up to about $1,200. In the previous hand, "Bob" had gone bust and re-bought another $500. I've played with Bob before and know that after a loss he is very willing to gamble in an effort to recoup his losses. True to form, the next hand he was dealt he raised pre-flop to $25. It was folded around to me, and I called with the A♣Q♣; we took the flop heads up. The flop brought a J♣6♣3♣; I had flopped the nut flush. Because Bob was likely to raise with almost any reasonable hand following a loss, I had little to go on regarding his holdings at that point. He then bet $25 into a $55 pot. I was now suspicious of a big hand because, while he bet, he bet a small amount inconsistent with the level of aggression I was expecting based on my observation of his play over time, particularly after going bust. In other words, this looked like a "please call me" bet. The range of hands I was putting him on at that point was an overpair or a set. I believed that, with any other hand, he would have at least bet the size of the pot. Again, this determination was based on my knowledge of this individual player; you've got to know your players.

I fully expected that he would pay me off if I raised, but if he did in fact have a set he would pay me off later as well. The other aspect of this hand, which is crucial, is that, if the board paired and he continued to bet, because he was on tilt at the moment, I wouldn't have been able to determine with certainty whether he was betting a full house or two pair with his overpair and would have found myself in a tough position. Raising to find out where I was at in the hand would have done no good because he would just have shoved all-in with either of those possibilities. I'd have made a small call rather than a large one if that scenario played out; thus, I wanted to keep the pot small so that his future bets would likely remain small.

Based on these factors, I decided to flat-call the $25, and there was now about $100 in the pot. The turn card brought a 4d, and he led out for $50, which I decided once again to call, with the idea of raising him all-in on the river if the board remained unpaired. The river brought an 8♥, and he bet $100. I raised him my remaining $300, and he beat me in the pot flipping over trip jacks. As a matter of fact, as he turned over his hand, he said, "I know you don't have the flush. You would have raised me long before this if you had the flush." Against another player in another situation I would have raised with the flush earlier, but since this player was absolutely going to call an all-in bet, regardless of whether it was made on the turn or the river, there was no point. I couldn't prevent him from drawing regardless of how I played the hand; had I raised him all-in on the flop, he would have called as well. When he called an all-in bet on the flop, he would have had a 34.5%

chance of completing, and I would have had to fade a 34.5% shot for all my money. Instead, I gambled $25 on the flop that he wouldn't draw out on me on the turn. I gambled $50 on the turn that he wouldn't draw out on me on the river. I put in $400 on the river when there was absolutely no risk.

If I'd gone all-in on the flop for my remaining $475, my expectation on the flop bet would have been as follows.

$$($9.50)(0.655) = $622.25$$

By keeping the pot small, I increased my expectation, though there are more pieces to consider.

$$($50)(0.655)+($100)(0.773) + ($800)(1.00) = $910.05$$

You may be wondering what would happen when he hits his hand by the river the other 34.5% of the time. Good question; let's take a look. Let's say the river brought a 3♦, giving us a board of J♣6♣3♣4♦3♦. The pot is $200 currently, and, based on how he bet during the actual hand, it's unlikely that he will bet any more than $100. Keep in mind that he bet only $100 on the river when a blank fell, and, based on his immediate call and his comment to me, he seemed to believe that there was no chance he was losing. In other words, believing himself to be holding the winner, he bet only $100. The board pairing wouldn't change that, so let's say that he bets $100 this time as well. I would have called the $100 to win $300 believing there to be a greater than 3:1 chance that he would have a hand such as K♥K♦ and would have lost a total of $200 on the hand. What I have done in this hand, by playing small bet poker, is to hold my losses to $200 during those times when he draws out on me while earning $500 during those times when he doesn't.

The second advantage gained from playing small bet poker is that you can often take a pot away from an opponent without risking a large number of chips. Because your opponents have seen you making or calling small bets with very strong hands, sometimes even the nuts, you are likely to get a disproportionate amount of respect from them while making or calling very small bets. Often, if I'm concerned that I may face a large reraise that would require me to fold, I can make a small bet that will often gain me a disproportionate amount of respect and, as a result, the pot.

Flopping a Draw

You call pre-flop with an A♠J♠, and the flop comes 9♠3♠6♦. How do you play it? There are many variables, particularly those concerned with your opponents and what their tendencies are, but let's say that you are in MP and have taken the flop five-handed with two EP players and two LP players. There is $25 in the pot currently, and each of you has approximately $500. If it's checked to me, I'm content to check along in such a situation. I don't wish to be put in a spot where I bet $25 and when it gets back to me I am facing a $200 reraise. I want to see this hand through to the end. In a bigger game, I might bet this hand and, if raised, go over the top; that is my style. In a smaller game such as this, however, it's not such a good move. The reason is simple. In a big game against better players, I may move someone off a hand as stong as JJ and certainly off a hand such as A9. In your typical LLNL game, however, I may be called by a hand as poor as A♦3♦ or 7♥7♠. My decision to call a bet is based on whether or not I feel the bet is likely to be raised, how much the bet is, and how likely it is that I will get callers behind me. These situations require you to have a good understanding of your opponents.

Let's say that I have a very straightforward player to act first who checks. Because he plays very straightforwardly, I expect that he won't check-raise if he calls at all. The two players behind me are calling stations and haven't thrown a hand away since Roosevelt (the elder) was in office. There is $25 in the pot, and the player to my immediate right, a fairly good player, bets $50. Do I call? The pot is laying me current pot odds of $75:$50 or 3:2. My current card odds to make my flush — I can't assume an ace or a jack will be good facing such a bet — are 9/47 or 4.2:1. Clearly I'm not getting anywhere near the right odds to call now, but I have two calling stations behind me who call everything. When they call, I will get $175:$50 or 3.5:1, and there is an offhand chance that the UTG player will call as well. Well, 3.5:1 is still not sufficient to make the call based solely on pot odds, but with implied odds I have more than enough reason to call, in great part because of the two calling stations behind me.

Usually when I flop a draw, if I feel I will get action, I simply check and call, assuming I'm getting the correct odds to do so. If I feel I can take the lead and bully people out of the pot, then that becomes an entirely different matter.

Types of Draws
Flush Draws
Straight-flush draws: I'll play a straight-flush draw very aggressively. An open-ended straight-flush draw with two overcards is a dream hand. If you are holding 9♥8♥ and the board comes 7♥6♥3♣, then you are a 51:49 favorite over a 5♦4♦ even though it's the current nuts. I'm prepared to get all my chips in with this hand and two cards to come, particularly if I'm doing the betting. I don't want to call all my chips off and, as a result, plan on being the one doing the betting with such a hand. With no overcards, the hand is not as powerful, but I will still play it very aggressively.

Nut flush draws: Typically the average LLNL player plays a nut flush draw as if she's in a limit game. If it's bet on the flop, she tends to raise for a free card on the turn and then will check the turn if she didn't make it. If she is first to act, she'll often bet the flop with her draw. Under normal circumstances (there are exceptions), these strategies are off base. Let's say there is $40 in the pot, you flop the nut flush draw, and you bet $40. What are you going to do if your opponent makes it $200? Many of your opponents will make such a raise with a lesser flush draw or even a straight draw with a flush draw present. There are, of course, the tighter players who won't bet or raise with their flush draws; you can usually figure out where they're at simply because, when they call, they tend to beat you in the pot with their call. Typically the flush draw bets the flop and then checks the turn if she misses. Personally, and against most opponents, I check the flop, and if there's no interest in the board I will often take a shot at the pot on the turn.

Small flush draws: I play small flush draws carefully. Typically I'll check and call as long as the pot is offering me sufficient odds to call. I tend not to figure implied odds because, even if I hit my flush, I will usually keep the pot relatively small if I'm at all unsure whether or not my opponent has a larger flush. Be attentive to the betting pattern of your opponent while the draw is present; he will usually alert you to what he has. Typically one makes a small flush draw while holding suited connectors. These types of hands can be powerful but not if a player insists on paying off the larger flush every time one is present.

Straight draws: Be very careful when drawing to any straight when a flush draw is present.

Open-Ended

Two overcards: An open-ended straight draw with two overcards is usually a powerful hand. For instance, if you are holding the J♠T♠ and the flop brings 9♠8♦2♥, then you have a hand that can stand some heat or, better yet, dish some out. I like to get some money in the pot early with a hand such as this so that I can increase the size of the pot for those times I do hit. This doesn't mean that you need to bet it; if you are in the pot with an aggressive player who will bet it for you, you can simply call along as long as you are getting the right number. I will bet such a hand only if those in the pot are passive players who are unlikely to bet, are even more unlikely to raise, and are capable of mucking.

Beware, though, a hand such as KQ with a flop of JT4. Such a hand fills the requirements of an open-ended straight draw with two overcards, but you lose the strength of your overcards with such a hand because you are more apt to be in serious trouble if you hit one. For instance, if you hit a king on the turn, you may find yourself facing a Q9 or an AQ.

One overcard: With one overcard, I slow down considerably. In the previous example, either straight you made would be the nut straight; here only one of two possibilities is.

No overs: With no overs, I look for a free card if I can get it. Unless the pot is very large in relation to a bet on the flop, or the implied odds are very high, I am prepared to release this hand. Essentially this hand has value only if the lower of the two cards comes, which brings the value of this hand down to that of a gut shot.

Double gutters: This is a very strong hand in which the strength lies in its deception along with its possibilities. For instance, if you hold the J♠T♠, and the flop brings A♣Q♥8♣, then you are holding the type of hand that busts people. Eight cards give you the nuts, and an opponent would be hard pressed to put you on such a deceptive hand if you get there. While I don't consistently bet my draws, as with an open-ended straight draw with two overcards, I like to get some money into the pot early with such a hand. While I'm content in the case of the open-ended straight draw, which also has eight outs, to allow someone else to do the betting for me, if I'm reasonably certain that I won't be raised, then I like to be the one doing the betting on the flop with such a hand to add to the deceptive value if I hit.

Gut Shots

Two overcards: With only four certain outs, this hand is played cheaply if at all except in those cases where the implied odds are very large. Typically I want to invest no more than about 5% of my stack with such a hand.[10]

One overcard: With the exception of an AJ or AT, it's difficult to find yourself in possession of such a draw. Other examples of this draw require hands that are usually unplayable under normal conditions. Under playable conditions,[11] you still require excellent implied odds.

No overcards: This hand can only call a check, and you must be very wary if you do make your hand. Typically, if the hand is checked on the flop and I make the straight, then I'll check it down. The only person you will bust by betting such a hand is yourself.

A word about tainted outs: a tainted out is an out that makes your hand but gives your opponent a bigger hand. The classic case is when a flush draw is present on the flop and you are drawing to a straight. Rather than having eight outs, you have six clean outs and two tainted outs.

---

[10] *Remember, my opponent must also have sufficient chips to give me the appropriate implied odds.*
[11] *Playable conditions would be against TPPs or players over whom you have very good control.*

When You're Both on a Draw

Let's say you decided to limp in and see a flop in late MP with the 5♦4♦. Six people took the flop, which came 7♥3♥2♣. On the flop, it was checked around to an LP player who bet $30, and it was folded around to you. This particular player, like many of his peers, will raise pre-flop with any pair, yet he didn't. Even if he is one of those players capable of limping with a small pair instead of raising, many of them believe that such a hand isn't vulnerable and will often check to give someone a chance to make something. Since he didn't raise pre-flop and then bet the flop, it's unlikely the flop hit him hard, so he probably doesn't have a set and is unlikely to be playing 73, 72, or 32 for two pair. The best this player is likely to have, then, is A7 or a flush draw. We both have $500.

There is nothing wrong with mucking in this spot. In fact, it's a pretty solid play. That said, if I'm playing against someone whom I'm able to read well, then I will occasionally set up to make a play for the pot. Reread that sentence and note the use of the word *occasionally*. Some players have a mission to try to figure out how to win every pot in which they are involved. That mind-set is a losing proposition. I have no problem with laying down a hand such as this, but for the purposes of mixing up my play I will sometimes make the following move.

I will call the $30, and if an overcard to the board comes on the turn I'll bet $30. If he hesitates, then calls, I will put him on a seven, and if another overcard falls on the turn I will make a large bet and take the pot. If he calls immediately, then I will put him on the flush draw. If I have put him on the flush draw, then I have only six outs to make my straight and 10 outs assuming, which I should, that an off-suit four or five will be good enough to win in a showdown. He has me beat currently, and I have only 10 outs to make my hand. The issue is not, however, whether or not he has me beat and how likely I am to make my hand. The issue becomes how many outs do I have to win this pot, and that number is likely large. Since I was able to put him comfortably on a flush draw, then almost any card that doesn't complete the flush simply requires me to bet in order to win.

You may be wondering how I can put him on one of these hands with conviction. Recall above that a caveat to this type of play is that you must be able to read your opponent well. Had I been playing against a player whom I was unable to put on a hand with conviction, I would have passed up the opportunity.

When an Overcard Comes

This is one of those cases where there are no definitive answers; this is about reading your opponent. That said, I am quick to throw away without a fight especially in an unraised pot. The most frustrating example of this phenomenon for most players is when they have KK and an ace flops. If the pot wasn't raised pre-flop and an ace comes, how much action can you possibly get from an opponent whom you have beaten? Remember, your goal in LLNL is to bust or double through your opponent. This can't happen with an overcard on board when you have missed your set. As for the raised pot — again, it's simply about reading your opponent.

Regarding the times when you have kings and an ace flops: many players are very reluctant to throw away a pair of kings in this spot. Perhaps they feel that kings are simply too strong a hand to throw away, but the value of the hand is simply relative. You wouldn't hesitate to throw away 66 if you began getting a lot of heat after a board of A24, and you shouldn't hesitate to muck those kings either.

Coordinated Boards and an Overpair

When you have an overpair such as AA–QQ and you get a coordinated flop such as T♥9♥8♠, you must use great caution. Most players are willing to risk their entire stacks with as little as a jack in their hands. Against a hand such as JT, AA is just about even money. While I am normally a strong advocate for aggressiveness even with hands that are worse than even money, this is always because the added equity you get from those times when your opponent throws away makes the situation profitable. This isn't one of those cases. Against typical LLNL opponents, you have no chance of getting them to throw this hand away. Proceed with caution. This is when being able to put your opponent on a hand becomes crucial. If you are at all in doubt, then it's better to throw away.

JT on the Flop

When the flop includes a jack and a ten, it creates a unique situation. When the flop brings a 7♦6♥4♠, it is completely understandable not to be overly concerned about an 8♠5♠ or a 5♣3♣. It may be out there, but one can hardly find fault with a player if he gets trapped with a pair of queens against such a flop; not so with JT on the flop. Just about every reasonable hand your opponents could hold benefits from a JT. Nineteen of the top 20 hands[12] give your opponent a straight draw, a pair, or better. Nearly 80% of the top 50 hands also do. Regardless of how strongly you hit your hand, this is one that you should play very carefully.

Since the most common error that LLNL players make, based on their levels of experience, is to call when they should fold, you'll get drawn out more often when there is a JT on the flop than you will with any other flop. While you should welcome rather than fear it when your opponents make errors, you will often negate their errors if you can't get away from a hand to which they incorrectly drew. For instance, if you held a JT, your opponent held the AQ, and the flop came JT2, then he would be incorrect to draw to a straight if you bet any reasonable amount. Perhaps he incorrectly identified an ace or a queen as an out when he called your pot-sized bet. If a king comes on the turn and you can't get away from your hand, then, assuming you both have enough chips remaining, he may be able to make enough so that his call becomes correct based on implied odds.

---

[12] *Top hands as defined in a 10-handed game.*

Beware the Blinds

A common error I see LLNL players make is refusing to respect power shown by the blinds when rags fall. In an unraised pot, most players will call with any two cards in the small blind, and of course the big blind gets a free ride, meaning he could have anything. I see both of the following situations arise constantly, each according to the blind's style.

There are five limpers before the flop, and the flop brings 3♦3♣6♥. The big blind comes out with a bet, and a middle position player who limped with 9♦9♥ raises to see where he is at. While he may certainly be facing a hand such as 6♠4♦, it's also completely reasonable that he is facing trips. This isn't normally a hand that you want to become involved in. Keep in mind that your object here is to bust your opponent or double through him; this isn't the type of hand you are likely to do so with. Consider who is more likely to go broke here, you or your opponent? He isn't going to lose all his chips with a 6♠4♦ on such a flop; will you lose all yours with a 9♦9♥?

The second situation is just a variation of the first because of stylistic differences in the ways various players play. For instance, you are holding 9♦9♥ before the flop and limped in. The board comes 3♦3♣6♥; it is checked to you, you bet, and the big blind calls. What do you think he has? This is the blind; he can and will have any two cards. In this particular case, he has two cards that he can call a bet with, out of position. At this point, you should be done with the hand unless a nine comes.

If this seems too simple a concept to even mention, take solace in the fact that you are playing in a game in which a raise by the blinds in a situation such as this often elicits a call by the original bettor. It's important to remember that most of your opponents in an LLNL game are going to play very straightforwardly or with very little deception. If the blinds are telling you that the rags on board hit them, trust them.

The Double-Paired Board

Often the board will be double-paired by the river or, less often, by the turn. This is a situation that almost all players play incorrectly. There are a number of principles that they ignore in making this error.

Let's take the following situation, which occurred in a $2/$5 game a few months back. I was dealt AQs in early position and limped. There was one additional limper, and the big blind checked; we took the flop three-handed, and there was $17 in the pot. The flop brought a QQJ. The big blind checked, and I bet $20; only the big blind called, and there was now about $55 in the pot. The turn brought another jack (QQJJ), and my opponent checked. What do you do? In almost every situation, you are correct to check. When I described this situation to one of my intermediate classes and told them that I checked, there were objections that could be heard outside the building. How do you check with the big full? I described the situation to them exactly as I described it to you here; are you wondering the same thing?

Here's what they didn't take into consideration.

- What type of player am I facing in the big blind?
- What range of hands have I put him on?
- What is the size of his chip stack?
- What is the size of my chip stack?

You'll note that I didn't discuss any of this in the above paragraph, nor did I mention it in class. Making a determination about what the correct course of action is prior to factoring in these or similar considerations is a major failing of most players. They have what they believe to be a no-brainer situation and proceed where angels fear to tread — at least this Angel.

Let's answer these questions and see where the answers lead us. The player in the big blind is my toughest competition at the table. He is a tight-aggressive and tricky player. Since he's a good player, what range of hands am I to put him on? Well, he limped pre-flop, which doesn't give me any information; he is capable of limping with anything, even AA. His pre-flop decision, then, doesn't help me. He called my $20 bet on the flop out of position, however; does that give me any information? It certainly does. Being a good player, he isn't going to call with a straight draw when the board is paired. He also knows that I'm a tough opponent. There is no doubt that he has a hand. He was in the blind, so he could have any hand that includes a queen or JJ, though if he had a queen with a poor kicker he would have bet out immediately to see where he was at or, at the very least, check-raised me for the same reason. Q3 isn't a hand that a good player is going to play slowly here. Therefore, I suspect he has a queen with a good kicker or JJ. I have the AQ, however, so his kicker isn't an issue if he does have a queen unless he's holding the QJ. As for stack sizes, he has about $600, and I have him covered.

As I said, when I told my class that I checked on the turn, they nearly came out of their seats. "How could you check queens full?" Good question. How could anyone check queens full? In other words, how could my opponent check queens full? If this is incomprehensible, then we must at least consider that he must not have queens full. However, our analysis led us to believe that he had a Qx or JJ; therefore, if he doesn't have queens full, then he must have JJ, or our analysis was faulty. I liked my analysis. I still do. Therefore, it was clear that a check was in order.

The river came an offsuit three, and my opponent bet $600 all-in. There is $55 in the pot. If my opponent does in fact have a queen, I will win half the pot or a whopping $28. Call $600 to win $28. For a call to be correct, he must not have JJ any more than once in 22 trials.[13] Clearly I can't draw that conclusion from the way the hand was played, and a pass is correct.

Besides failing to take into account all the factors inherent in this hand, the class forgot our filter: "Who, as a result of this action, is more likely to go broke?" In this case, I was much more likely to go broke by calling than was my opponent.

This example was based on knowing my opponent to be a tight-aggressive, tricky player; what if he wasn't? Well, our analysis of his range of hands would be different. A loose-aggressive player, for instance, wouldn't check the big blind with JJ or even AQ, KQ, or QJ, so I would have known I had the best hand on the flop based on a lack of a raise pre-flop. Yet I said that this is a situation that almost all players handle incorrectly despite the fact that I may have called a loose-aggressive player in this spot. The error isn't the call or the fold. The error arises in the thinking process that gets you to your decision. If you routinely fail to take the quality and type of your opponent into consideration, as well as stopping to analyze what range of hands he could have and the size of your chip stacks, then you are making an error.

---

[13] *This assumes that this particular opponent will never be bluffing here, which, incidentally, I believe is true. Even if he was prone to bluffing on the rare occasion, the pass would still be correct. The risk-to-reward ratio is simply too highly based on the likelihood of him having JJ based on our analysis.*

Avoiding Situations in Which You Are Drawing Dead

In the previous chapter, I described a hand in which I said of my opponent, "Being a good player, he isn't going to call with a straight draw when the board is paired." This is typically a situation that, as the saying goes, separates the men from the boys. You almost never see a good player put in any money, particularly in a small pot, trying to make a hand when he is possibly drawing dead, yet you see inexperienced players do this constantly.

Here are some common situations in which we may find ourselves drawing dead.

1. Drawing to a straight when a bigger straight than the one we are drawing to is already possible.
2. Drawing to a straight when a flush is possible.
3. Drawing to a straight when a full house is possible.
4. Drawing to a flush when a full house is possible.

There are two principles that should guide our actions in such situations.

1. The object of no-limit is to bust your opponent or double through him.
2. Who, as a result of this action, is more likely to go broke, me or my opponent?

Here you won't bust your opponent unless he plays very poorly indeed. If he plays that badly, then there will be more opportune spots to take his money, and you don't need to perform this dance to get it. A typical opponent won't put all his money into the pot with a hand that you can beat when even your hand can easily be beat.

For instance, you are holding the QJ, and the flop comes T99. If the flop is checked around and a king falls on the turn, how do you like your hand? Let's hope you didn't see the flop with someone who asked himself, "Who, as a result of my checking my tens full of nines, is more likely to go broke on this hand, me or my opponent holding a QJ?" Whom are you going to bust in this hand? Do you think you'll bust someone holding an AK? Again, if your opponent plays so poorly that he would give you substantial action with a board of T99K while he is holding AK, then you should pick a better spot. He may be willing to go all-in with AK, but as they say even a blind squirrel finds a nut once in a while, and he may have accidentally picked up K9.

Don't pay to draw to a hand that may not be good if you get there. If you get a free card and complete your draw, continue to check. If your opponent makes a small bet on the river, then you may want to call depending on the opponent, but don't invest heavily in this pot.

Nuts with a Free-Roll

There will be cases in which you have the nuts with a redraw. For instance, you have the A♥J♥ in MP, and the flop comes A♣K♥T♥. Let's say that three people saw the flop for $15; there is $45 in the pot. The early position player makes it $45, and let's say both you and the late position player call, bringing the pot to $180. Now the turn brings a Q♦. You now have the nuts and the nut flush redraw. Many players in this spot will try to string their opponents along. This isn't the spot to do so. If your typical opponent is holding a jack at this point, then he won't have the knowledge or the discipline to throw away the nuts at this point, and it's important to get the full house draws out. Bet the farm. There is $180 in the pot, and if you have $2,000 left then you should bet $2,000. Incidentally, if you have only the straight at this point without a redraw, and your opponent overbets the pot, then for the same reason you should almost certainly get out despite having the nuts right now.

If your opponent does have the redraw, then this is what you are facing: there are nine cards that could give your opponent a flush out of 45 unknown cards.[14] This means that you are calling to win $90, which is your half of a split pot, and you will lose one time in five (nine times in 45). Assuming that your opponent went all-in for $400, you'll make $90 four times for $360 and lose $400 once. Unless you are short-stacked enough to overcome your opponent's free-roll, you should pass. This should illus-

---

[14] *We are counting a jack as a semi-known card because we are acting on the belief that he also has the straight.*

trate, too, why it's important not to try to "string your opponents along" in this spot. By betting too little, you can create a situation in which it's correct for your opponent to call. For instance, in the above example, if your opponent went all-in with less than $360, it would be correct for you to call. Keep in mind that in the above example, what would make a call correct is that your opponent went all-in; if he had more chips in reserve, then you might want to pass as well. If he bet a mere $70 or less in an effort to string you along, then you would be correct to call regardless of how much he had in reserve.[15]

This situation is usually much less costly in LLNL than it is in a traditional no-limit game simply because the sizes of the stacks don't often reach an amount necessary to make calling an error. This is one of the many ways in which LLNL artificially protects inexperienced players.

[15] Actually the figure is $72, which is 80% of $90. This, of course, is dependent on knowing that he had the redraw. Since it's unlikely that you would know that with certainty, you'd often be willing to call more, but the point remains that the player with the redraw should make it as expensive as possible.

Follow-Through Is Critical

So many aspiring players take the first step: they raise pre-flop to $25 with a hand such as AQs. Then the flop misses them entirely, and they end up checking the hand down or folding when someone bets because that someone realizes the pot is just lying out there, and no one wants it. Often the aspiring player says to himself, "See, raising in a game like this makes no sense. The muppets don't know enough to throw away." And so they revert back to their regularly scheduled tight-passive, losing game.

Some take it a step further. A player raises to $25 before the flop with AQs. He gets two callers. There is $75 in the pot. The flop of 8♦4♣2♥ misses him, and he bets $75. One player calls. The turn is the 2♣, and he decides that he should check. The pot is checked down, and the caller shows an 8♥7♥ and takes the pot down. And once again the aspiring player is left talking to himself about how badly his opponent played before he reverts back to his normal game plan.

You play the hand this time, but this time don't let up. Yes, your opponent just called $75 with top pair, poor kicker, but what does he think you have? He doesn't know. He has no clue. Putting you on a hand isn't a priority in his game plan. Make it one. Make a pot-sized bet on the turn or the river, and he'll have to consider what you have. While his analysis isn't likely to be complete or scientific, it will give him time to let his fears get the best of him. You don't do this indiscriminately, of course; you have to take your opponent into consideration, but, if your opponent wasn't one to throw away on the turn when you bet $225, then you should never have bet the $75 on the flop unless you had the goods.

That said, there are some times not to follow through or to change the way you follow through. If the turn card pairs the highest card on board, I'll usually check it to my opponent, but if he checks behind me I am firing on the river regardless of what comes. If I have position on him, then the situation reverses. If the highest-ranked card on the flop pairs on the turn and he checks to me, then I'd likely check behind him, but if he checks to me on the river then I'm going to make a pot-sized bet. He may check to you on the turn to check-raise you, but if you check and he checks the river as well then the pot is yours for the taking. The reason for betting this hand on the river against typical LLNL players is simply because they aren't strong players. As a result, they may have called your bets with a hand such as A2, A4, or 33 — all of which beat you. Therefore, you continue firing at them until they give up.

In a bigger game against strong opponents, I'd check this hand down at this point, by the way. Most tough players (particularly if the money is deep, which isn't going to occur on an LLNL table normally) would call your $75 bet on the flop with a 53, 56 — in other words, they might call your bet with a strong draw. They might also call your $75 with a set. These are both likely possibilities. They normally wouldn't both call your $25 pre-flop raise and your $75 flop bet with a nonpair hand that included a two or a four. Therefore, if you bet on the river, they would call you only with a hand that can beat your AQs and fold every time you have them beat.

Minimizing Risk against a Calling Station

Although I've recommended aggressiveness often throughout this book, there are times when discretion is the better part of valor. A case in point: I've limped with AJo, I've taken the flop four-handed, and there is $20 in the pot. The flop comes A♣J♠7♠. A straightforward and predictable player in early position bets out $20, and it's folded around to me. I decide to raise to $80, and he calls immediately. We both started the hand with $300. Let's stop for a moment and review the likely scenarios.

He entered in early position but didn't come in with a raise. Since he is a straightforward player, we can assume that his bet meant he had a piece of this flop, most likely an ace. When I raised him, I wasn't reraised but called immediately. The immediate call usually represents a draw. If he didn't have a draw, he would have to consider whether or not his kicker was any good, but there was no hesitation because he knew he was drawing to the nuts. A suited ace is definitely a possibility, but not AK or AQ, because he didn't raise pre-flop. I will usually put a straightforward, loose-passive player on an ace with the nut flush draw. The turn card comes a 6♥. The board now reads A♣J♠7♠6♥.

Many, if not most, LLNL players will call any bet with a draw to the nuts. Because of this, if I make another pot-sized bet on the turn, which would be $180, he'll call with his top pair and flush draw. He shouldn't call based on my holdings and the size of the bet, but he will. Since he is willing to make the mistake of calling when he should be folding, I should punish him by betting, right? Well, not quite so fast. He started the hand with $300. He called $5 before the flop and put in $80 on the flop and $180 on the turn for a total of $265. He certainly should call his last $35 on the river even if he misses and thinks that he is beat, because the pot will be $580, and I have to be bluffing only one time in 15 to make the call correct.

Let's try this scenario. If I am correct that he is on a flush draw, he will check the turn to me if the flush does not come. He has $215 left. What if I bet another $80? He will call, of course; we just made the determination that he would call $180 on the turn, so certainly he'll call $80. If he misses on the river, then he will likely call me on the strength of his aces if I bet his last $135 on the river, particularly since the $80 wasn't a very strong bet on the turn. Many opponents, if I check the turn, will put me on an inferior flush draw and take my check to mean that I was on a draw and missed, allowing me to bet the entire $215 on the river and still get a call on the strength of his aces because he believes me to be bluffing.

So which strategy should you use against this type of opponent? Let's look at sample results. In the first scenario, you committed $80 to the pot, and if a flush comes on the turn and he bets you off the pot then you can muck for the minimum, losing $80. The flush will come 19% of the time on the turn, which we'll treat as one in five for simplicity's sake. The other 81% of the time the flush won't come on the turn, and you'll be faced with a decision. Assuming you know your opponent well enough to realize that he will call each of the following bets, let's see what your highest expectation is.

Bet the size of the pot: $180. He will make the flush on the river approximately one time in five. On those occasions when the flush doesn't come, you simply bet your opponent's remaining $35, and he calls. On the one occasion in five that the flush does come, if you are lucky enough to have him check to you, then you should check as well, losing $180.[16] This play has a positive expectation of $136.[17]

Bet $80 on the turn when the flush doesn't come. If the flush doesn't come on the river, bet $135 on the river. This play has a positive expectation of $156.

Check when the turn brings a blank and bet or raise all-in on the river if the flush doesn't come.[18] This play nets you a positive expectation of $172.

This type of play only works against a weak player, but there are many of them in the LLNL games. I use variations of the above example many times a night. Using such a technique even two times per eight-hour session can increase your hourly expectation by $10. This type of analysis demonstrates a powerful concept in playing winning poker. It's very easy to become complacent when you are employing a strategy that has a positive expectation already. Often, though, behind a good strategy lies a great strategy waiting to be uncovered. Look for it.

---

[16] *It is unlikely of course that your opponent will check if he has made a flush, and it is equally unlikely that you will be certain enough that he has the flush for you to throw away a $575 pot for $35. His betting would lower your expectation even more.*
[17] *At the time of the turn bet, there is $180 in the pot. While it's true that if you win you'll win the $180 in the center, we are looking at a strategy for the turn and river bet only, so I am calculating expectation from the turn onward during the 81% of the time in which the turn did not bring a flush.*
[18] *Only if you are certain that your opponent will call on the strength of his aces. If you aren't certain, then this play is a poor choice.*

The Semi-Bluff

Earlier in the text we examined how to calculate our chances of making a draw based on determining our card odds and compared that to our pot odds in order to determine whether we had sufficient chances to make our hand to justify calling. We then examined implied odds and saw how, even if we didn't have sufficient pot odds right now, our implied odds may have justified a call. This covered those purely mathematical situations in which we were calling.

When we bet or raise instead of check and call, however, there is another variable that affects our odds. This variable, while mathematical in nature, can't be arrived at mathematically; it is a psychological variable, and we must know our opponents in order to calculate it. When we call a bet, we have one way to win; we must show down the best hand. When we bet or raise, however, we have two ways to win: we can show down the best hand, or we may win the pot uncontested if our opponent fails to call.

The concept of betting or raising when you don't have or don't believe you have the best hand right now but have a chance of improving to the best hand on later streets is called the semi-bluff. To determine whether a semi-bluff is profitable, we must be able to calculate the chances that our opponent will muck if we bet or raise.

Let's take a look at an example. Let's say that you are holding the 6♣5♣ and a very tight player raised UTG to $25. You both have $500 in front of you. You put him on one of three hands based on your experience with his particular brand of tightness: AA, KK, or AK.[19] You know then, within an acceptable range, what he has, and, furthermore, he doesn't know what you have, so you have that advantage over him. You also have the advantage of position over him. As a result of these factors plus the $500 in front of him that you are salivating over, you decide to call, and the flop comes 8♠4♦2♣. Because he's a tight, conservative player, it's likely that he bets AA or KK and checks AK in this spot. Let's say he bets $50 or the size of the pot. The pot is offering you $100 for a $50 call or exactly 2:1 at this time. Since it's reasonable that he will bet the turn as well, you need to calculate your outs based on one card to come. You have eight chances in 47 unknown remaining cards, or you're about 5:1 against.

Let's look at implied odds next. Since you are 5:1 against, you'd have needed $250 or more in the pot to justify calling based on pot odds or $250:$50. This means that you have to be confident that you'll extract another $150 out of this player on the turn if you do make your straight in order for a call to be correct based on implied odds. Because this player is very tight, it's highly likely that, if you call this flop bet and he doesn't improve on the turn, he will check. If you bet $150 on the turn, it's likely that he will fold even with AA or KK.[20] If he won't pay you off when you make your hand, then you aren't getting the implied odds to call either.

[19] *Such a narrow range of possible hands for your opponent is not necessary; the play works even with a player who has a broader range of possible hands as long as it is still a definable range.*
[20] *Although it may be possible to bet $75-$100 on the turn and again on the river, thereby extracting enough to make a call correct on the flop based on implied odds, we will ignore this possibility this time in order to illustrate the power of the semi-bluff.*

If you call when you are getting insufficient odds, then you'll go broke. It's just a matter of time. Calling is clearly not a good option. You would have to be playing very loosely to make this call, and loose play is not winning play; you are a tight player. So what must you do, fold? That would be tight all right — tight-passive. Passive play is not winning play either; you are an aggressive player. So of course you should at least consider a raise.

Let's examine that possibility. You have a double gut-shot and a backdoor flush draw or about 10 outs.[21] You are about a 3:2 dog with two cards to come. In other words, you have about a 40% chance of winning this pot by the river based on your cards. Let's say you call the $50, making the pot $150, and raise $450. If he calls the $450, then you have actually put in $500 to win $600 — his remaining $450 and the $150 that was already in the pot. So $500 to win $600 is still not good enough to justify the raise when you have only a 40% chance of winning this pot. Forty times out of 100 you win $600 for a total of $24,000, and 60 times out of 100 you lose $500 for a total of $30,000. You're down $6,000 in 100 tries, which comes out to a negative expectation of $60 per occurrence. So does this mean that raising is incorrect? Certainly not.

You mustn't forget that your opponent is a very tight player. By raising $450 into a $150 pot, you make it unlikely that he will call with one pair, even if that pair is

---

[21] *I am counting a backdoor flush draw as one out and the combination of two running fives or sixes or one five and one six as an out. This isn't precise, but I often do such estimates at the table if I'm going all-in with two cards to come. The actual percentage with two cards to come is 36.9%. Nine outs with two cards to come is 35%, and 10 outs with two cards to come is 38.4%.*

AA. While every opponent is different, it's likely that he will throw away to this raise as much as 75% of the time or even more. Assuming, for the sake of our calculations, that he will throw away 75% of the time, we can now recalculate our expectation: 75 times out of 100 you will win $100 for a total of $7,500; 10 times out of 100 you'll win $600 for a total of $6,000; and 15 times out of 100 you'll lose $500 for a total loss of $7,500, giving you a net of $6,000 in 100 trials or a positive expectation of $60 per occurrence.

The power of the semi-bluff lies in the times when your opponent throws away the best hand. Some opponents will throw away like clockwork when you raise on a semi-bluff, while others will doggedly pursue you. Against these latter opponents, the semi-bluff isn't effective.[22] In the above example against a calling station, for instance, you'd maintain a negative expectation.

---

[22] *This isn't always true. If your semi-bluff bet or raise causes your opponent to check the turn, giving you a "free" card, then it may also be profitable.*

When to Slow-Play

Slow-playing is normally defined as when you have a big hand and choose to check or call rather than bet or raise in order to elicit future bets or calls from your opponent on a later street. In big bet poker, however, the size of one's bets isn't fixed, which allows a player another possibility to slow-play. An example from a typical $2/$5 game should show this situation clearly.

Let's say a tight-aggressive player in early position raises pre-flop to $20; there are three callers and $85 in the pot. The flop brings an A♠K♦7♥, and the tight-aggressive player checks. If you were one of the pre-flop callers, cards aside, would you want to make a bet at this point? That is a very dangerous flop considering that a tight-aggressive player in early position raised. Because such players are by definition aggressive, I'd find his check to be more disconcerting than a bet. With no flush draw and an inside straight draw at best, this might seem to many to be an ideal time to slow-play a hand such as a set of aces or kings. An experienced player who understands this might bet in order to try to give the illusion that nothing is amiss. He wouldn't want to bet so much that he'd lose the field, but he might bet an amount that would be both easy to call and lead someone to believe that he isn't very strong. If our hero had KK, for instance, and bet $40 into an $85 pot, I'd consider this to be slow-playing as well.

Therefore, let's amend our definition to read "slow-playing is defined as when you have a big hand and choose an action that belies the true strength of your hand in order to elicit future bets or calls from your opponent on a later street."

Now that we've defined slow-playing, let's not use it. I'm not a fan of slow-playing in LLNL for two important reasons. First, because of the very large implied odds possible in big bet poker, slow-playing has significantly more risk than it does in a fixed-limit game. Second, and more important, everyone slow-plays today. There was a time when you could sit down at a game and only a few expert players were using slow-playing as a tool. This is no longer the case. Anyone who has watched a couple of episodes of poker on television is looking for the dramatic moment in his own game where he too can slow-play.

There is no reason to slow-play if your opponents would call; as a matter of fact, what slow-playing usually does is keep the pots you win smaller because you didn't get in that extra bet. Because so many players expect to see a slow-play, it can be more effective to bet out your big hands immediately. This may seem contradictory to my discussion regarding small bet poker, but this isn't the case. In our discussion on small bet poker, we chose to make small bets when we felt that our hand was vulnerable. In the instances we are examining now, it's the very act of slow-playing that makes one's hand vulnerable.

Let's take a closer look at the above example. Let's say the tight-aggressive player did, in fact, have KK with a flop of A♠K♦7♥. Let's say, too, that both he and his opponent had $500 in front of them. By betting $40 into an $85 pot, he is allowing an opponent to call cheaply with QT, QJ, or JT and try for a gutshot with the proper implied odds to do so.[23]

---

[23] *The opponent would get the correct odds only if you are willing to lose the rest of your chips if he makes his hand.*

Because your typical opponents would slow-play when they flop big hands, they not only expect you to slow-play but also can't fathom why you wouldn't. This is an example of the egoistic fallacy that Alan Schoonmaker discusses in his book *The Psychology of Poker*. There is a second reason that an immediate bet is your best strategy in an LLNL game that is based on the level of experience of your typical opponent.

Most LLNL players are new to the game of hold'em. Remember, LLNL wasn't around even a few short years ago. Recall, too, that one of the most persistent fears of inexperienced players is that they are going to be bluffed. When you put these reasons together, you get an internal dialogue that goes something like this: "There's no way he's got that; he wouldn't bet it if he did, he'd try to trap me or check-raise me or something. . . . He must be bluffing!"

Many players resist the idea of betting immediately and believe they should slow-play much more than is profitable. So let's look at an example and see what happens. You are dealt the A9 in the big blind. There are three callers, and you take the flop four-handed. The flop comes AA9; what do you do? Most of my students tell me that they would check. I ask them why, and they tell me that they're hoping their opponent makes something. Uh-huh. So I ask, "Like what? What can possibly come on the turn that is going to make an opponent, who has nothing now, sit up and start liking his hand after a flop like that?" Then we have a moment of silence. Eventually someone points out that someone could have a pocket pair such as TT or perhaps even an ace. Great! Then what are we waiting for? Let's bet our hand! Then someone else points out that the last time he bet in a situation such as this everyone threw away. Okay, so they threw away. What types of hands would someone throw away in a spot such as this? KQ maybe? What exactly is capable of landing on the turn that would make KQ call a bet? In other words, they throw away now or they throw away later, so what's the difference? On the other hand, since players would expect you to slow-play if you had an ace, when you bet your hand out you are more likely to be called or even raised by those players who think you must be bluffing.

Now is the time to slow-play. If I have bet out and been raised by someone who either has a hand or thinks that I'm bluffing, then I will usually slow-play and just call. Depending on the player, I may lead out on the turn (if I believe that he won't bet again) or check to him, allowing him to bet.[24]

Other times to slow-play include when your expectation increases by slow-playing, such as the example in the section "Minimizing Risk against a Calling Station." One's expectation doesn't automatically increase by slow-playing. As with any tactic in poker, spending time thinking about situations and working out problems away from the table are the keys.

[24] *Among the factors that would determine how I play the turn is how deep we both are.*

When to Give a Free Card

I consider giving a free card to be an entirely different situation than slow-playing. I have defined slow-playing above. The time to give a free card, by contrast, occurs when

> (1) your hand isn't strong yet figures to be the best right now;
>
> (2) your hand is unlikely to be beaten by giving a free card;
>
> (3) you aren't likely to get a call currently; and
>
> (4) by giving your opponent a free card, he is likely to think you are stealing when you do make a bet on a future street; hence, he will be more likely to call.

All of these criteria need to be met before giving a free card becomes profitable.

This isn't a move I am likely to make against tough competition, but there are a lot of weak players in LLNL whom you will be able to put on a hand with a good degree of accuracy. An example would be when you have a hand such as K♠Q♠ and a predictable weak player raises pre-flop. Let's say that you can, by having observed his play, accurately put him on either a pair or a big ace. Let's also say that this player plays very straightforwardly with little or no deception. This type of player abounds in LLNL, and you'll find that this particular situation comes up frequently. If the flop comes A♠Q♦3♥ and he checks to you, then you know that he has a pair that isn't present on the board.[25] Against many players, such as the one I

---

[25] *While it is possible that he is trying to slow-play, as we discussed in the previous chapter, he would certainly not check the turn to you if this was the case.*

described, he will fold to a bet, putting you solidly on an ace. If you check, though, this type will often think that you are trying to steal or semi-bluff if you bet the turn, particularly if a spade, diamond, or heart comes, which would put up a flush draw.

If he checks the turn as well, then he has two outs to beat me with one card to come, and I will usually make a reasonable bet at this point, say $40 into a $50 pot. I will usually get a call. Because this player plays very straightfor-wardly, he will almost always come out betting on the river if he connects and will almost always check if he misses. The pot now has $130 in it, and I will make another small bet here trying to get him to call. By "small" I mean usu-ally $25–$40, and I'll vary that amount based on the size of the river card. The smaller the river card, the more I'll bet; the higher it is, the less I'll bet. Your opponent is con-cerned about a bigger pair than what he has and will be more likely to call another $40 if a card falls that is smaller than his pocket pair. If the river puts another overcard out there, then you can usually entice him with a bet smaller than the bet you made on the turn. This is usually seen as suspiciously reminiscent of a steal attempt, and more often than not you'll get paid off.

The Check-Raise

Check-raising, along with slow-playing, shares the title as the most overused tactic in poker. There is no doubt that check-raising has its place in poker, but it is used so indiscriminately that often whatever advantages a player gains when it's appropriate to use the check-raise are lost while he is busy using it inappropriately.

The most common use of the check-raise is when a player wishes to get more money into the pot when he wants a call. This goal would be better served in most cases by betting the hand out directly. Consider the following common situation taken from a $2/$5 game.

It is folded around to late position, where you make it $20 with the A♠Q♠. A typical opponent in the big blind with 9♠9♣ decides to call. There is $40 in the pot. The flop comes A♣9♦8♥, and he checks his set looking for a check-raise. A $40 bet from you would be reasonable, with the expectation of picking up the pot right there. Your opponent, however, calls the $40 and raises $120. What do you do? Of course, you immediately try to put him on a range of hands based on this new information — he has a hand that he feels is strong enough to check-raise you $120 with. While each player has his own standards, one pair isn't among those standards for all but the wildest players; you have to assume two pair or a set. Having done so, you muck, and your opponent earns $40 post-flop.

Compare this to the situation where the big blind

comes out betting $40 on the flop. You have a reasonable expectation with top pair, good kicker, that you have the best hand and raise to find out, perhaps calling the $40 and raising $120. Let's say the big blind reraises you all-in your last $120. If you throw away now, the big blind makes $160 on the flop, four times as much as he would have if he had check-raised you.

Every time there is action at the table it conveys information to the player who is listening. If I bet, then I am basically saying I think I have a good hand based on the limited information at that moment. If you raise me, then you are basically telling me to "get it fixed," that my hand isn't good enough. If I check, then I am saying I'm weak. If I then check-raise you, I am screaming "HA! I'VE GOT YOU!" and even most inexperienced players can hear that, causing them to fold.[26]

---

[26] *Experienced players will often bet inconsistently with the direct strength of their hands in order to make use of deception. The meaning behind each of the actions listed above is strictly basic communication and doesn't address more advanced deceptive plays.*

Playing against a Short Stack

Most players with a short stack are scared that they will go broke. As a result, they play in a way that almost guarantees they will. They fold hand after hand before the flop, blinding away the remnants of a once proud stack. If they do limp in, usually a sizable raise will get them to reconsider, and they will fold. An exception to this is players on tilt, but they would almost never limp in anyway. If they do see the flop, however, be aware that most players will make a desperation call if they are severely short-stacked. If there is $150 in the pot and your opponent has $20 left and checks to you, this isn't the time to try to bluff any but the most timid players. Keep in mind, too, that even the most timid players are likely to be encouraged to call by the other players at the table who want to see what you have. Now, they aren't allowed to do this, but once someone at the table says something it can't be unsaid. If you complain at the time or remind them of the rules, then it may appear that you don't want a call, and the player will be encouraged to call as a result. Checking down a poor hand against a desperately short-stacked player who had enough of a hand to call your raise before the flop isn't a bad policy if you have very little. Most of the other players at the table, aware of your aggression and thinking that you are always bluffing, will think twice the next time you make a play at them if they see you check down top pair with a mediocre kicker.

Often you get into a situation where your opponent didn't begin the hand short-stacked, but since the hand began he has become so. Let's say you started the hand with $500, and your opponent began with $220. Your opponent entered the pot from EP with a raise to $20. There were three callers when it got to you on the button, and you called with 7♣6♣. You took the flop four-handed, and it brought a 4♣3♥2♣. The field checked to you, and you decided that a semi-bluff, pot-sized bet of $80 was in order. The EP raiser considered a moment, then called, and the rest of the field folded. There is now $240 in the pot, but, more importantly, your opponent has $120 left. This will play a significant role in determining how much you should bet.

We discussed a similar hand earlier, but that was a case in which we knew we had the best hand. In this case, we know we don't. Actually the only hand we can beat at this time is a 75. Because your opponent raised pre-flop and then checked the flop after taking a moment to consider, we can be fairly confident of his holding at this point. What is the range of hands the typical player would have at this point? Against the typical player at LLNL who raised pre-flop in EP, I expect to see a hand such as AK and not an AK of clubs. If he held the A♣K♣, he would have called more quickly, perhaps even bet it himself with the combined strength of two overcards, a flush draw, and a straight draw. Incidentally he would have been correct to do so. Against even a hand as powerful as top set, he would be only about a 2:1 dog. With the $80 in the pot already, it would be more than reasonable for him to make a pot-sized bet here.

Back to our example, though, we expect our opponent to have an AK, perhaps an AQ. He is beating us at this point and has made a poor call. Some of you might think he has made a good call because he has us beat at this point, but it simply isn't true.[27] Since he doesn't know what

---

[27] *You may believe that, according to Sklansky and the Fundamental Theorem, he hasn't made a mistake, but had he seen our cards he should have raised.*

our hand is, he believes that he must hit an ace, a king, or a five for him to win. Since he believes he has 10 outs, if he is correct about that, then he is incorrect to call, since the pot isn't laying him the right pot odds. Implied odds won't bail him out either since he can't expect to get much action if a five or an ace comes*, either of which makes a straight possible with one card.

Now, having built the pot to $240, we need to use caution in determining our bet on the turn if we don't improve. Recall that we will be winning with a club, a five, a six, or a seven. We have 18 outs. On the flop, we had a 62.5% chance of hitting our hand, with two cards to come. If the turn card comes a blank, say an off-suit ten, then we need to be very careful. We still have 18 outs, but if our opponent continues to believe that an ace or a king is going to save the day for him then he's likely to call our bet now since he called so readily on the flop when we made a pot-sized bet. Now he doesn't have to call a pot-sized bet, simply because he doesn't have that much left. Betting $120 to put your opponent all-in is now a poor idea against your typical opponent. Since he still believes he has 10 outs, he is under the impression that he is approximately a 3.5:1 dog to win the hand, and the pot is laying him 3:1 on a call. He's unlikely to be figuring this out, of course, since his previous call indicated a lack of calculating, but it will likely "feel" more right to him. While he would still be incorrect to call considering the pot odds and his analysis, he already exhibited a willingness to make a more grievous mistake on the flop when he was getting only 2:1. If he is willing to make an error of

*unless he is beat

that magnitude, calling when he is getting 2:1 and his chances of making his hand are 3.5:1 against, then he is unlikely to be concerned about 3:1 odds and will call this bet too. The obvious problem with this is that he has us beat, and we will lose if we don't improve. Because he has us beat at the moment, and because he will call if we bet, it's better to check at this point and save that bet for the river. On the river, unless a nonclub ace or a king comes, a $120 bet should secure the pot for us because there's nothing left for him to draw to.

This particular player's shortcoming was his willingness to draw at a hand that may not be good if he hits it while not getting sufficient odds to do so. Because he is a loose-passive player but not a pure calling station, he won't call on the end with nothing, so we must rearrange our bets and change the nature of our aggression, saving some of that aggression for the moment when he will back down.

Playing against a Big Stack

Most players don't like playing against a big stack. They are concerned that they will get pushed around, but it doesn't have to be that way. In fact, playing correctly, you can often push around a big stack with a small stack. If you have a small stack, then you can choose opportunities to go all-in when you are guaranteed certain odds and have the opportunity to improve even further. Let's say that an aggressive player under-the-gun with a large stack makes it $20 to go in a $2/$5 game. There are three callers, and you are on the button with an AK and $100 left. If you choose to go all-in at this point, you are getting approximately 2:1 from the pot, with one caller almost guaranteed, and any further callers only increase the odds you are getting. For instance, if all the remaining players call, then you are getting 4:1 on your $100. If the aggressive player reraises to $400 and everyone folds, then you have increased the price you are getting from the pot to about 3:1, and you face a more limited field with no extra monetary commitment on your part because you are all-in.

On the other hand, a large stack always[28] must be concerned that he will face less favorable odds down the betting line. Using our example above, what if the UTG player decided to call your raise and the next player decided to raise $400 more? It's very likely at this point that the UTG player will be forced to fold, and you'll be seeing a flop for your original investment. I'm not terribly fond of being matched up against a player who thinks a $400 reraise is a really great

[28] *Actually there are two exceptions. If the large stack closes the action, then this isn't true on that betting round. Also, if no one is left with enough to raise behind him, then he doesn't have to face decreased odds.*

idea, but there is good news. If I'm up against QQ or JJ, then I'm a 1.3:1 dog while getting about 2.4:1 from the pot. Even if I'm up against KK, then I'm still only about a 2.3:1 dog while getting 2.4:1 from the pot. Neither of these situations has a negative expectation, and while I am normally looking for better odds than this but with a short stack I'll take what I can get.

Consider the following two situations.

I have J♠T♠ in the big blind in a wild game. I also have $500 in front of me. The blinds are $1/$2. UTG comes in for $10. When it gets back to me, there are (including me) eight callers. I raise $90 more. Fold, fold, call, fold, BANG — the other big stack at the table raises $400 more, putting me all-in, and it's folded around. I must fold too, losing $100. You may be asking yourself why I'd raise $90 with a J♠T♠.[29] Well, if I eliminate the field, I win the $80. If I eliminate half the field, I am less than a 2:1 dog against three random opponents while getting nearly 4:1 on my money. Let's say I get three callers, and then another player who shares the distinction with me of having the smallest stack calls his remaining $90 with AA. Certainly one of the worst situations I could face. I'm 4.5:1 against winning this pot against AA and three random hands, and the pot is laying me just about 5:1, which is still a positive EV situation.

Now let's try this situation. You have J♠T♠ in the big blind in a wild game. You have $100 in front of you. The blinds are $1/$2. UTG comes in for $10. When it gets back to you, there are (including you) eight callers. You raise $90

---

[29] The fact is I wouldn't if I had $500 in front of me. The next example needs this one for comparison. Although I wouldn't make this play in any situation I can imagine, there are still advantages that I go on to describe.

more all-in. Fold, fold, call, fold, BANG — the big stack raises $400 more, and it's folded around. In the worst-case scenario, you are up against aces, and you are a 3.6:1 dog, but you are getting $250:$100, which, while still losing, isn't losing nearly as much as I've lost, because you've still got about a 22% chance of winning. In the previous example, I had a 0% chance because I had to muck. But of course he probably doesn't have aces. He likely would have raised the first time around, particularly with $50 dead money in there already, so what is he likely to have? AK off-suit, maybe? Maybe a small pocket pair? Those are my guesses against typical players. So what are the odds there? Against an unsuited AK, you are about a 1.4:1 dog but are getting 2.5:1 on your money with a positive expectation of $43.92 every time you play that hand, that way, against AK off. And I lose $100 every time I play the same hand with a big stack because I'm forced to muck. What about a small pocket pair? How about 55? Here you are a straight-out favorite at about 0.9:1 while getting 2.5:1, so your positive expectation on this matchup is $83.54, while my expectation is still -$100. And all this because you had a small stack instead of a large one.

Now, granted, there are times when your short stack will cost you, but my point is that there are positive and negative aspects to playing any size of stack; you simply must adjust your play to compensate and play to the strengths of whichever you have. Playing with a short stack need not be a disadvantage unless you try to play it like it's a big stack.

Playing a Small Stack

I don't recommend playing a short stack, but if you find yourself in such an unenviable situation there are ways to optimize your chances of building it up. First of all, don't blind yourself broke. You have to get in there and gamble even if you aren't a favorite to win; all you want is sufficient equity.

Let's say you were playing $2/$5 blind LLNL. If you find yourself desperately short-stacked with $20 in front of you, there is a raise to $20 or more, and there are four callers when it gets to you, then you should call, regardless of your holdings. In a game of this nature, the big blind is almost certain to call as well, and even if no one else does you are still getting 6:1 on your money.

If you are desperately short-stacked (i.e., $20), and it's been folded to you in middle position or later, then go all-in — again regardless of your holdings. Since you may win the pot right then and pick up the blinds, which would provide a 35% increase to your stack, it's worth a try. Is this sound poker strategy? Hardly. However, since you are in a tough spot without sound alternatives, this is making the best of a bad situation.

If you are short-stacked but not desperately so, then your strategy changes somewhat. Let's say you have $100, and the rest of the table has $300 or more. Again, if you can get 5:1 or even 6:1 or better on your money, then it may be worth a call regardless of your holdings, especially if the game is aggressive and you are prepared to re-buy. However, with that exception, your play changes. If there are a number of limpers, and you are in late position with any kind of hand, then be prepared to raise sufficiently to fold the field. If there are six limpers when it gets to you, then a raise that folds the field increases your chip stack 35%. If you are called, you may still hit a hand. If you think there's a chance you may be called, then consider raising to $20, with the plan to go all-in on the flop if it's checked to you.

Don't slow-play or limp with a premium hand. Get full value and raise. If you have AKs, and are in MP or later consider raising $100 all-in, particularly if there are limpers already. Calling a $95 raise is only likely to come from a person who either shares AK with you (which is horrendous; she should muck) or has a pocket pair, and unless she has AA or KK you are a coin flip to win while getting better than 1:1 pot odds because of the dead money in the pot.

Again, these types of plays aren't optimal. Far from it. Why, then, am I recommending them? In a perfect world, you'll never become short-stacked, but if you do you'd just pick up AA, and it would hold up. Yeah, that's gonna happen. If you make no changes to your style, then you will almost certainly go broke; good hands just don't show up that often. These suggestions are designed to give you a fighting chance, but they aren't substitutes for replenishing your stack the old-fashioned way. If you play better than your opponents, then you'll be much better off buying more chips.

Playing a Big Stack

Having a large stack in low-limit no-limit has a number of advantages.

> 1. You don't need to worry that someone will sit down and buy enough chips to cover you, thereby negating your advantage.
> 2. You will be able to maximize your potential when your opponent makes a mistake.
> 3. You will be able to bully the table and often "put the question to your opponent" for all his chips while not putting your stack in any serious jeopardy.

When you have the table covered, you have a huge advantage. An added benefit when playing low-limit no-limit is that no one can take this away from you artificially by simply buying enough chips to cover you, as he can in a traditional no-limit game.

Furthermore, when your opponent makes a mistake in no-limit, it can cost him all his chips, but only if you have enough to cover him. Opportunities to bust someone don't come up every hand, and it's extremely disappointing to find yourself short-stacked when an opponent is trying desperately to go broke in what is surely going to be your pot.

In no-limit, it's a huge advantage to be able to "put the question to your opponent" for all her chips. If you have a commanding chip stack, then you are able to do this far more frequently. Someone with $100 in front of her is far more likely to call a $20 all-in bet than a bet that costs her the entire stake. This provides you with more bluffing opportunities.

Since having the big stack at the table allows you to bust anyone in a single hand, players who enter a pot with you understand that they risk going broke, so most players need to have a better starting hand than their usual requirements in order to get involved in a hand with you. Even if they see a flop with you, many players simply fold to a bet on the flop too often to have a chance to win. If your opponents are tightening up against you when you have a big stack due to their risk of going broke, then by all means take advantage of this by betting more frequently.

Less frequently players will loosen up against you, trying to quickly double up through you by gambling, sometimes with any two cards. If you tighten up too much against this type of player, then he'll show an automatic profit, and you'll have to get in there and mix it up on occasion. If such players are short-stacked and keep putting themselves all-in every time you are involved in a pot, then your game plan simply becomes waiting for any pair or big ace. Then, if you can get them alone, by all means oblige them. If they are going in with any two cards, then you are a favorite to have the best hand. While I'm not a big fan of gambling, there are two advantages to this tactic. First, your chip stack isn't in serious jeopardy, because they simply don't have enough chips to cause you a problem; second, those tighter players at the table who don't want to gamble will see that you are prepared to do so and may tighten up even more against you.

Short-Handed Play

Playing short-handed can be your most profitable time at the table. Many players avoid short-handed play, and, to tell the truth, they probably should because most players don't know how to make the necessary adjustments from a full-ring game. The most significant change in short-handed play over a full game is that hand values change dramatically.[30] Also, aggression is rewarded even more than it would be normally. Against most LLNL players, short-handed play truly is like taking candy from a baby. If your opponents are unable to adjust to the changed hand values and are playing passively, then you should be raising most hands. If it's raised before it gets to you, then you will need a very strong hand to continue, because their raising values usually haven't changed from what they were during a full game. Normally, when I'm playing in a short-handed LLNL game, my (pot-sized) raise either wins the pot immediately or gets one caller. When I say "normally," I mean better than 80% of the time, and it's about 50-50 whether I get the caller or win it immediately. This means that a solid 40% of the time I win the blinds and that another 40% of the time I must contest the pot. If you hold two different ranks in your hand, such as A9, then you'll flop a pair or better only about a third of the time. Two-thirds of the time the flop will miss you. With that figure in mind, regardless of what I have, I will normally bet the flop, and two-thirds of the time my opponent will have missed,[31]

---

[30] *See Appendix B for complete comparison of changing hand values.*
[31] *While it is true that your opponent may flop hands that don't require pairing his hole cards, such as a straight or a flush, this is offset by the fact that he might also flop second or third pair and not believe that his hand is strong enough to continue.*

and I will take down the pot. Of the one-third of the time that he does hit something, he simply may not have enough that he feels justified in calling a pot-sized bet. And I will hit a hand on occasion myself, even if he does. Since I'm winning the blinds so often, I almost always straddle in a short-handed game. In a $2/$5 game, the straddle is $10. There are two benefits to straddling for me. First, I have last action, and if the game is four-handed then I maintain excellent position over any callers except the button. If the game is three-handed, then I'm the button. Second, I can usually encourage the other players to straddle, which means there's more money in the pot for me to win. Since I'm winning the blinds such a high percentage of the time — if I've gotten the other players at the table to straddle as well — I am winning $17 each time I win the blinds instead of $7.

Short-handed play can be difficult to learn well. The fluctuations are larger than in a ring game, so it can be difficult to determine if you are being outplayed or having a normal, large fluctuation until you have lost a great deal. You should, as noted earlier, be playing even more aggressively than you normally do. If your opponents are playing aggressively as well, then they may also have a good idea of how to play short-handed, and you'd do well to choose another game. Prior to sitting down at a short-handed game, study the appendices in this book that deal with changing hand values.

Chapter 7

Four-Way Examples

These examples indicate a typical play or series of plays that I would make in each situation. Not everyone fits neatly into one of these categories, and even among those players who do they don't always play identically. These examples also don't take into account information I've been able to collect from watching and listening; they are stock responses and as such have certain limitations. They do, however, show a range of responses based on basic player types. In each of the following cases, I have asked myself how I would play against a specific opponent who fits the profile type in question. The player I have chosen to represent — a tight-passive player, for instance — won't play precisely the way all tight-passive players will play, but you will find similarities. When examining the following situations, you should look for patterns and tendencies, not memorize the exact plays.

Often I am asked questions such as "How do you play

AKo from EP?" or "Is 99 worth a raise in this position?" The answer is always "It depends." Poker educators and authors have been stymied in their efforts to explain the "It depends" clause to new students, and I hope that these examples help to break through that wall.

Example 1

- $500 — $2/$5 blinds, **7♣6♣**
- An early position player raises to $20. I call in middle position, the field folds, and there is $50 in the pot. We both have $500.
- Flop — **4♦5♣8♥**

LPP: The loose-passive player will normally check a hand such as AK and bet a big pair with such a flop. Despite being passive, most players will bet a big pair. If this player checks, then I will bet $50–$60, expecting a call. A bet and call of $55 will put the pot at $160. He will likely check the turn to me regardless of what comes. If he does in fact have AK and an ace or a king falls, then I will be able to bet more. Since he raised up front and checked the flop, this is the hand I'm putting him on.

Let's look at both situations. If an ace or a king falls and he checks, then I will bet about $175, slightly overbetting the pot. This will put $250 of the $500 he started the hand with into the pot with a near guarantee that I will get the rest on the river. If a blank falls, then I'll bet something more along the lines of $125 into the $160 pot, slightly underbetting the pot. This player is looking for a reason to call, and my underbetting the pot is often all the reason he needs. A bet and call of $125 brings the pot to $410 and leaves him with $300 — if an ace or king falls on the river, then I'll bet it all. If a blank falls, I'll probably bet $100-$120. I'll be betting less than the previous round. That looks suspicious, which again is all the excuse an LPP needs to call.

If he bets the flop, then it will likely indicate an over-pair, and usually the bet will be about $20-$30. If I call him, he'll likely put on the brakes, being a passive player, so it makes no sense to wait; I'll raise here and now. If he's bet $25 into the $50 pot, then I'll raise somewhere in the vicinity of $75–$95. Although he's a loose player, I don't want to risk losing him by betting too much. Because $100 is a complete stack, it's a psychological barrier to many recreational players. Let's say I bet $85 and am called. There is now $270 in the pot, and he has $370 left. Because this player actually has a hand right now, I can get the money in the pot more quickly than I could when he simply had AK. On the turn, I'll make a pot-sized bet of about $275. I'll bet $275 and not $270 simply because, if a scare card comes, even though I don't think I'm going to lose him, I want him to have less than $100 left to make it that much easier to call.

TPP: With a TPP, I'll play the hand quite differently. With this player, too, I'll expect to see AK or a big pair — usually AA or KK. Most TPPs restrict themselves to raising in EP with these three hands. Against the same flop, this player will undoubtedly check an AK and bet AA or KK.

Let's look first at the case where he has AA or KK. This type of player can't take much heat, so I won't raise him but will simply call. Let's say that he bet $50 on the flop. That would put $150 into the pot. Incidentally, this type of player is more likely to bet the size of the pot when he bets. The turn will either hit him or not, but either way he'll likely bet $150, though there is the possibility that if he turns a set he'll go all-in, content to win the $150 right then; clearly, I'd call if this occurred. Now, TPPs are notorious for checking on the end; after all, you've called them all the way, and their tightness is fundamentally a function of fear. Usually, then, this is the last bet you can expect. After a $150 bet and call, there is $450 in the pot, and that's plenty big for a TPP. Because this bet leaves him with $280 left, and $280 is a mighty big number for a TPP to call all at once, I'll break it up for him by raising on the turn the minimum: another $150. In this way, I've left him with only $130 and have increased the likelihood that I'll get a call on the end as a result.

Now let's look at the case where he has an AK. He doesn't like this flop but figures you can't have any of that garbage; the flop is only eight high, and though he's pegged you as one of those aggressive lunatics who don't care anything about money it's still difficult for him to fathom anyone calling a raise with such cards. It won't make him bet, but you'll probably get a small call out of him, say for $30. If he doesn't improve on the turn, then he's prepared to be done with the hand. I'll bet another $30, or even $25, if necessary, whatever it takes to keep this particular player in the pot. Again, on the river, if he doesn't improve, then I'll make a $20 bet, even though I don't have high hopes of getting called by an unimproved hand. My only chance is to continue dropping my bet. He'll assume that he's beat, but this constant lowering of my bet while the pot continues to grow gives me a chance to frustrate him into calling.

LAP: Against an LAP, I can't put her on such a tight range of hands. She literally could have anything. She compensates me very well for this, however, by being willing to call most bets with little or nothing. It's almost certain that she will bet the flop. The only exception would be when she flops a very big hand, such as a set, in which case she may check and go for a check-raise. Let's look at those cases where she bets first.

If she bets, then it may be anywhere from $50 to $100. I'll raise her the minimum. If she has any piece of the flop, then she is likely going all-in right now, and if she has as little as a single overcard then I'll still get a call.

Let's say that she checks, though. You may find it strange that I will check here too. Recall that she will only check if she has a very strong hand. She may have the same hand as I do or a set. I'm going to wait for the turn. She's got a 35% chance of filling up if she flopped a set, and since she's so willing to get all her chips into the pot I'll wait and see what comes on the turn. If the board pairs on the turn and she bets, I'll throw away. I realize that I may be throwing away the same or a better hand, but I'm not going to risk $500 to discover that I get my money back. If, on the turn, the board fails to pair, then I'm going to get all my money in. She won't check this hand twice. The first time took all her self-control, and she may need counseling after that trauma. She will bet now, probably $50–$100. Usually I'll call and make certain that the river doesn't pair the board. She'll bet again, enough for me to put the rest of my chips in without fear of her folding. You may ask why I wouldn't put the rest of my chips in on the turn when I was an overwhelming favorite. The reason, quite simply, is because I can get all of her chips into the pot when I have a lock — why risk it when you are only a 77.5% favorite when she is willing to give you all of her chips when you have a 100% chance of winning?

TAP: Against a TAP, I will have some difficulty putting him on a hand. He will usually raise with fewer hands than the LAP, but he is still very unpredictable. That, coupled with his aggression, makes it very difficult to get the best of this player. Considering the game texture, though, will assist you in placing him on a hand. If the game is rather loose, then he is more likely to have a premium hand. If the game is rather tight, then he is more likely to be splashing around with less than premium hands. Let's look first at the situation where he bets into you.

The pot is $50, and he bets $50. Usually, and in the absence of any other information, I will raise another $100 here. Most players place too much emphasis on slow-playing against a good player. A good player knows that raising is often just a way to gain information and is often less concerned about a raise from you than a poor player would be. I expect a call. The turn, however, is a different matter entirely. He may check or bet. If he bets, then I will simply call here. A bet from a TAP in this spot will likely be $150 or so. He is still trying to get information, and, if you were trying to steal, he is going to make you pay. A raise here indicates that you have a legitimate hand, and I'm not ready to let him know that yet. If, on the other hand, he bets $250 or more, then I might as well put him all-in; he's got $75 or less left and will be very nearly forced to call. Incidentally, his being "very nearly forced to call" is a function of my unpredictability not being irrationally pot-committed.

If he checks the flop to me, then I'll go ahead and bet out. He expects this from me, and his check doesn't necessarily indicate an unwillingness to call. I'm going to bet somewhere in the vicinity of $75. It's overbetting the pot a bit, but I expect a call if not a raise. If he calls and bets the turn, then it will probably be in the vicinity of $150. In most cases I would just call this bet; a raise here would simply show too much strength against what is most likely a value bet on his part. If he checks the turn, then I'll usually check right along with him and try to collect on the river.

Example 2

- $500 — $2/$5 blinds, **A♠K♦** UTG
- I limp for $5, and it's called by two people before a late-position player raises to $30.
- Flop — **4♦5♣8♥**

LPP: Because this player is loose-passive, I have to believe that he has JJ or better. As a function of his passive playing style, he is unlikely to raise with anything less, with the exception of AK. I have at best a split or coin flip, and I may be very far behind, out of position against a loose player who won't lay down against aggression. In other words, I've got to have the best hand. As a result, I'll usually fold pre-flop.

TPP: The tight-passive player is also very unlikely to have anything less than a premium hand. Again I suspect AA–JJ and/or AK. Against this player, however, I'll call. Because of his tightness, I should be able to take this pot away unless the flop hits him solidly. On the flop, I am the first to act, and I will check. Unless he has AK, which is the least likely hand I suspect he has, he will bet his overpair. My check was partially for information and partially to set him up for a possible steal on a future street. There is $75 in the pot, and I would expect a bet of $50–$75, let's say $60.

While mucking is certainly not a bad play at this point, there may be another, more profitable option. If, for instance, I had good control of the table, then there's another possibility available to me that I will often make use of. Understand that this isn't an "every time play," but I will play the hand the following way rather frequently. I will minimum-raise another $60, and he will most likely call. In the unlikely event that he raises, I muck immediately. There is now $315 in the pot, and he has $350 left. I mentioned, in the introduction to this exercise, that I will try to give answers without taking into account the information I've gathered from listening and observing at the tables, but in this case it's imperative that I watch his call of my raise. If he calls easily, I'm done with the hand. His call, however, figures to be tentative. TPPs are fearful players, and they see worst-case scenarios all the time. If he looks uncomfortable calling the $60 raise, then I will do one of two things on the turn. If a ten or lower comes, I will go all-in. If a jack or higher comes, I will check. I may have the best hand if an ace or a king falls, but I will check nevertheless and watch to see his reaction to the card. I would beat JJ and QQ at that point, and if an ace came I would beat KK, but he's going to tell me what he has by his response to my check. He's already concerned because he got check-raised on the flop, so this turn card will have to give a set to get him going again. If he bets, then I'm done with the hand. If he checks after a jack or higher comes, then we'll usually go to showdown without a bet. This may appear weak, but he won't call a hand he can't beat, so it makes no sense, if I feel that I have the best hand, to bet a hand he won't call. This particular hand is a difficult one to script without being able to watch my opponent. I rely on tells, and TPPs are emotional critters who wear frustration on their sleeves.

LAP: Against a loose-aggressive player, out of position as I am, I will simply call pre-flop. She figures to have a wider range of hands than either of the two players whom we've seen thus far. A likely but by no means exhaustive list of possible hands she may have includes any pair and AK, AQ, AJ, AT, all suited or not, and Axs. Upon such a flop, I will check and fold. I may well have the best hand right now, but LAPs are so willing to give you their money that there's no sense getting involved in this hand with them when you have nothing. Pick a better spot.

TAP: Against a TAP, I will smooth-call as well, but I'd likely bet $50 on the flop. If raised, I'd simply muck. If called and I receive no other information, I'd check on the turn if I got no help, and if bet into I'd fold. With so many players at the table willing to give you their money, there's no reason to pick a fight to fill your rack. The TAP will make you fight for it.

Example 3

- $500 — $2/$5 blinds, K♠Q♣
- There are three limpers to me in late position; I raise to $35. There is one caller in middle position.
- Flop — K♦4♥8♠

A word on the raise here. I raise frequently and for a variety of reasons. While I may have the best hand right now, I realize that any ace has me beat. I do like to take control of the hand whenever possible, however, and with my position I'm poised to do so. Also, this is the type of raise I'd make with AA or KK, and if you restrict yourself to such a raise only when you are holding such a limited range of cards, observant players will soon catch on — this is just a way of mixing up my play. Furthermore, if I hit a flop, then I prefer to take this hand heads up. It's easier to determine the likelihood of one person hitting two pair or better after he has called a $30 raise than it is to determine the holdings of four opponents, including the big blind, who could have anything.

LPP: Based on this player's profile, the call of my raise means little. However, this is a particularly good flop for my hand, and about the only thing that's going to get me off this hand is if this player bets into me. LPPs don't want to annoy anyone, and as a result he wouldn't want to slow-play a set (88 or 44) or K8♠, which are the only hands I'd be concerned about. So, yes, against a true LPP, I throw away if he bets the flop, but he is very unlikely to do so. So, facing a check, I make a pot-sized bet of $85. I may well lose him here based on the size of the bet, but I'm not going to give him a cheap draw with a 75o, K2♠, 98o, or any number of unlikely hands that I can't put him on. If he calls and checks the turn, he will face an almost automatic pot-sized bet unless an ace, eight, or four shows up. In any of these cases, your knowledge of your opponent and your ability to read him are going to come into play.

TPP: I'm not thrilled with this player's call. I do have position on him, but he may well have limped with AQ♠ or even, though less likely, AK. More than likely he has a medium pair such as 99, TT, or JJ, but I will remain cautious of the AK possibility. I received a good flop for the hand and am relatively confident that I have the best hand.

I considered AK to be the least likely hand he is holding and still do. If he bets, I will fold, but I expect a check. A bet on my part at this time is likely to lose him, and I'll win the $85 pot, but usually here I'll check behind him. This may surprise some of you, but if he has one of the hands I put him on then he is drawing very slim. With AQ, he's got three outs, and with any of the pairs he's got two each. If a baby comes on the turn, then I'll probably be able to get another $50 out of him and perhaps again on the river. He won't give me credit for a king if I check behind him on the flop, so if he tries to put me on a hand then he'll often come up with AQ or a pocket pair smaller than a king. I'm not suggesting that he should put me on such a holding, just that after I check on the flop most TPPs whom I play with will.

LAP: Against a loose-aggressive player with position, I feel pretty confident with this flop. If she bets into me, I will raise. If she had AK before the flop, she would have reraised me had she somehow forgotten to raise the first time action got to her. If I'm raised back, I'm going to have to consider the likelihood of two pair, because with a pocket pair she likely would have raised pre-flop as well. If she checks the flop to me, then I will bet the pot — $85. With any pair, reasonable draw, or even some unreasonable draws, I'll expect a call. On the turn, if she improves, then she will undoubtedly try to take the lead, and I will usually release the hand. Otherwise, regardless of what comes, she's going to face another pot-sized bet, this time $255. If I don't win it right here, if she checks the river to me, then I'll bet the $125 she has left. If she bets into me on the river, then I will call.

TAP: Against a TAP, I really like this hand. He limped

pre-flop and then called my raise out of position, which really defines his hand for me. I don't put him on AK. Although I suggest it, most TAPs will rarely limp with this hand. I have position on him, and his hand is easier to define than that of most player types. While 44 or 88 is a possibility, I won't usually have to concern myself with hands such as K8, K4, or 84. If he bets into me, which he may, particularly if he has a king, I will usually flat-call. He will be trying to define my hand, and I'm not going to alert him to the strength of my hand quite yet. If he checks, then I will bet the pot — $85. It doesn't do much to define my hand yet, simply because he expects me to bet here. I raised pre-flop, and I'm an aggressive player.

Let's examine both a raise and a call. A raise on his part of $85 is usually a feeler bet and indicates a king with a suspect kicker, perhaps a queen through ten. I will call this and prepare to go all-in on the turn if it's checked to me. A big check-raise, while possible, is suspect coming from most TAPs; it's a bit early to be dropping the hammer on me if he truly does have a big hand, but I will still lay it down against most opponents.

A flat call, however, puts me into my shell. He will likely check to me on the turn, looking for a check-raise if he flat-called the flop, and I will check behind him; TAPs are not callers. If he checks/calls, then it signifies danger.

Conclusion

What you have in your hands is a primer on low-limit no-limit. This book contains everything you need to become a knowledgeable player. Unfortunately it won't make you a great player — or even a good one. Only you can do that. Fortunately for you, most people are looking for a short-cut. Don't take one. Read the book. Study it. Wear the cover off it so that you need to buy another copy.[1] Take all the quizzes. Work on problems away from the tables, discuss the game with your friends or join an online forum, take notes, do what it takes.

---

[1] *Ignore this. An author occasionally has to say something that'll make the publisher happy.*

Glossary

All-in	All-in refers to pushing all your chips into the pot.
Baby	A baby refers to a small ranked card.
Backdoor	A hand made in the last two cards. E.g., "Joe had a backdoor flush draw" or "Joe back-doored a flush."
Belly buster	An inside straight draw.
Blank	A poor card that has no impact on the hand. Also called a rag.
Bluff	To bet strongly with a poor hand, as if you have a strong hand, in an attempt to make others fold.
Board	The community cards in a hold'em game.
Bust	To lose all of your chips or cause another player to lose all of his chips.
Call	To match the current high bet.
Calling station	A player who almost always calls and seldom raises.

Calling time	A request for additional time to make a decision to call, fold, or raise.
Check-raise	To check at first, then raise should anyone else bet. This is done as a way to lure other players into betting when you think they may fold if you bet outright.
Cold-call	To call both a bet and a raise.
Community card	A card dealt faceup on the table that can be used by any player at the table.
Connectors	Pocket cards of sequential rank.
Drawing hand	An incomplete hand such as four cards to a straight in which you are drawing cards, hoping to make your hand.
Dominated	A hand is said to be dominated if it has three or fewer outs against another hand. E.g., AK dominates AQ because the AQ can only win with one of the three remaining queens.
Double belly buster	A draw that includes two gutshot straight draws. E.g., you hold JT, and the flop is AQ8. You will make a straight with a 9 or K.
Double gutshot	See double belly buster.
Double through	Doubling through an opponent occurs when you go all-in and win against a single opponent, thereby doubling the size of your stack.

Draw	You have a draw if you need a card or cards to complete a hand.
Early position	Early position refers to the first three positions after the big blind in a full game.
EP	Early position.
Expectation	How much money a decision is worth on average.
Flop	The first three community cards.
Flush draw	If you have a four flush with cards to come, you have a flush draw.
Fold	To give up on your hand and any chance to win the pot.
Four flush	Four cards to a flush.
Gutshot	An inside straight draw.
Heads up	A pot that is being contested by only two players. Can also refer to a game in which only two players are involved.
Implied odds	The odds you are getting from the expected calls in future betting rounds.
Inside straight	A hand in which you have four cards to a straight but are missing one in the interior. E.g., you have JT, and the flop is AQ2. It would be said that you have an "inside straight draw."
Late position	Late position usually refers to the button and the position to the immediate right of the button.

Limp	To limp is to come in for the minimum pre-flop.
Low-limit no-limit	A no-limit game that has a maximum buy-in.
LP	Late position.
Middle position	Refers to the fourth, fifth, and sixth positions after the big blind in a 10-handed game.
Min raise	To raise the minimum amount allowed.
MP	Middle position.
Muck	The pile of folded and burned cards in front of the dealer. Also, to throw away one's hand, as in "Joe mucked his hand."
No-limit	A poker structure in which a player may bet any amount of chips (from the minimum allowed up to all the chips she has) when it's her turn to act.
Nut flush	Highest possible flush.
Nuts	The best possible hand given the cards on the board.
Nut straight	Highest possible straight.
Off-suit	Cards with different suits, usually referring to hole cards.
Open	Make the first bet in a round.
Open-ended	A hand with four cards of consecutive rank. A straight can be completed by drawing the fifth card at either end. E.g.,

if you have a JT and the flop comes 982, then you can complete a straight with a seven or a queen. You have an open-ended straight draw.

Outs	Any remaining card that will give you the winning hand.
Overcard	A hole card higher than the highest card on the board. E.g., if you have AK and the flop comes 963, then you have two overcards.
Overpair	A pocket pair higher than any card on the flop. E.g., if you have QQ and the flop comes 963, then you have an overpair.
Paid off	Calling someone's bet when the caller is losing. e.g. Joe paid Mary off.
Pocket pair	Two cards of the same rank in the hole.
Post	To put in a blind bet, often required when you first sit down in a cardroom game or change seats.
Pot equity	That portion of the pot that represents your expectation.
Pot odds	The ratio of the amount of money in the pot to the amount it will cost you to call the current bet.
Probe bet	A bet intended to discover where one is at in the hand.
Rag	A poor card that has no impact on the hand.

Rainbow	A flop containing three different suits.
Raise	To increase the amount of an opponent's bet.
Rank	The numerical value of a card.
Represent	To have the appearance of a certain hand. E.g., if the flop brought three hearts, then a heavy bettor might be said to be representing a flush.
Reverse implied odds	They apply to those situations in which the pot odds appear to be better than they truly are.
Ring game	A full standard, nontournament poker game. Also called a live game.
River	The last card dealt in a game.
Rock	A tight and passive player who folds often and doesn't play a lot of hands.
Scare card	A card on the board that could mean a monster hand for someone.
Second pair	A pair with the second highest card on the flop.
See	To call.
Semi-bluff	To bet a hand that doesn't figure to be the best hand at the moment but that has good odds to improve to become the best hand.

Semi-known card	A card that hasn't been seen yet but can reasonably be accounted for by an opponent's play.
Set	Three of a kind when you have two of the rank in your hand and there is one on the board.
Short stack	Having fewer chips than a typical player at the table.
Showdown	When all cards have been dealt and betting is complete, player hands are revealed in a showdown.
Slow-play	When you have a strong hand, to indicate that you have a weak hand to encourage others to bet.
Straddle	An optional extra blind bet, typically made by the player one to the left of the big blind, equal to twice the big blind. This is effectively a raise and forces any player who wants to play to pay two bets. Furthermore, the straddler acts last before the flop and may "reraise."
Straight draw	Another number of draws in which you can make a straight with the next community card.
Suited	Cards of the same suit.
Suited connectors	Sequentially ranked hole cards in the same suit.

Tell	Something a player does that gives away the strength of his hand.
Tilt	To play wildly or recklessly.
Top pair	A pair with the highest card on the flop.
Trips	Three of a kind when you have one of the rank in your hand and there are two of the rank on the board.
Turn	The fourth community card. Also known as "fourth street."
Under-the-gun	The position of the player who acts first on a betting round. Also known as UTG.
Value bet	A bet based not on the intrinsic value of your hand but on the relative value of your hand versus those of your opponents.

Appendix A

Quiz 1

I

1. J♦T♦	6. A8	11. K♦x	16. 5♦x
2. T♦6♦	7. A7	12. Q♦x	17. 4♦x
3. 6♦5♦	8. 99	13. J♦x	18. 3♦x
4. A♣A♥	9. 88	14. T♦x	19. 2♦x
5. A9	10. 77	15. 6♦x	20. JT

II

1. 6♠6♦	6. 63	11. T6	16. AJ
2. JJ	7. 33	12. 6x	17. KJ
3. 99	8. A6	13. AA	18. QJ
4. J6	9. K6	14. KK	19. JT
5. 96	10. Q6	15. QQ	20. TT

III

1. 88	6. Q8	11. 8x	16. KK
2. AA	7. J8	12. AQ	17. Qx
3. QQ	8. KT	13. AJ	18. Jx
4. JJ	9. T9	14. AK	19. TT
5. A8	10. K8	15. Ax	20. 99

IV

1. J♣8♣	6. Tx	11. Q♣x♣	16. 4♣x♣
2. 8♣6♣	7. 99	12. J♣x♣	17. 3♣2♣
3. T♦T♥	8. 7x	13. 8♣x♣	18. J8
4. 7♠7♦	9. A♣x♣	14. 6♣x♣	19. 86
5. T9	10. K♣x♣	15. 5♣x♣	20. AA

V

1. 9♣x	6. JJ
2. 6♦6♥	7. TT
3. AA	8. 88
4. KK	9. 77
5. QQ	10. xx

VI

1. KT	6. 99	11. Q7	16. 97
2. T8	7. 77	12. Q5	17. 95
3. 86	8. 55	13. J9	18. 75
4. QQ	9. QJ	14. J7	19. AA
5. JJ	10. Q9	15. J5	20. KK

1.	KJ	6.	44	11.	A2	16.	T2
2.	53	7.	22	12.	QT	17.	42
3.	AA	8.	AQ	13.	Q4	18.	AK
4.	QQ	9.	AT	14.	Q2	19.	KK
5.	TT	10.	A4	15.	T4	20.	KQ

VIII

1.	5♠5♥	6.	54	11.	AA	16.	AJ
2.	QQ	7.	44	12.	KK	17.	KJ
3.	JJ	8.	A5	13.	AQ	18.	Jx
4.	Q5	9.	K5	14.	KQ	19.	TT
5.	J5	10.	5x	15.	Qx	20.	99

IX

1.	QJ	6.	99	11.	K7	16.	97
2.	J8	7.	77	12.	K6	17.	96
3.	8x	8.	66	13.	T9	18.	76
4.	KK	9.	KT	14.	T7	19.	AA
5.	TT	10.	K9	15.	T6	20.	AK

X.

1.	K♦Q♦	6.	TT	11.	A♦x	16.	3♦x
2.	Q♦x	7.	99	12.	K♦x	17.	2♦x
3.	7♦x	8.	J8	13.	6♦x	18.	KQ
4.	8♠8♥	9.	T8	14.	5♦x	19.	Qx
5.	JJ	10.	98	15.	4♦x	20.	7x

Quiz 2

1. There are open-ended straight draws (KQ, Q9, 98) and gutshot draws (AK, AQ, K9, Q8, 97, 87). There is also a club draw.
2. This example has two flush draws, both spades and clubs. It also has a double gutshot draw with a 76.
3. There is a diamond draw.
4. This example has no draws.
5. There is a spade draw. There is also a double gutshot draw with a 54.
6. There are open-ended straight draws (98, 85, 54) and gutshot draws (T8, T9, 95, 84, 43, 53).
7. There are open-ended straight draws (T8, 86) and gutshot draws (J8, T6, 85).
8. There is a double gutshot draw with a QJ.

.

9.   There is a spade draw.
10.   Any card that doesn't pair the board completes a straight. There is each type of straight draw represented here as well as a heart draw.

Quiz 3

1. 10 — You have to beat a pair of tens. You have a gutshot draw and can beat his pair of tens with a jack, of which there are four. You can also beat his pair of tens with either a king or a queen. Since you have one each, there are three of each left.

2. 21 — You have to beat a pair of eights. You have an open-ended straight draw, a heart flush draw, and two overcards. There are nine hearts unaccounted for that would complete a flush, three nonheart sixes and three nonheart jacks that would complete a straight, and three nines and three tens that would give you a bigger pair.

3. 11 — There are nine spades that would give you a flush, but the ten of spades would give you a flush while giving your opponent a full house, so we can't count the ten of spades. That leaves us with eight spades and three nonspade queens to complete a gutshot straight.

4. 10 — You have three aces that would give you a better hand than your opponent as well as seven hearts remaining since your opponent has two of them in his hand.

5. 7 — Since your opponent has the straight, you must make a hand better than a straight. You can make either four of a kind with the remaining nine or a full house with either the three remaining eights or the three remaining sevens.

6. 10 — You have the same seven outs that you had in the previous question, but now you can also make a full house with one of the three remaining sixes.

7. 10 — You can complete the open-ended straight with one of either four fours or four nines as well as make three of a kind with the remaining two sevens.

8. 4 — You have a gutshot straight draw and will complete with any of the four fours.

9. 8 — You now have a double gutshot and will be winning with either a four or an eight.

10. 11 — You have a spade flush draw and a gutshot straight

draw. You will be winning with one of eight spades (the king of spades will give your opponent a full house and therefore isn't counted) or one of the three nonspade jacks.

Quiz 4

1. You have nine outs. The ratio is 38:9 or about 4:1.
2. You have eight outs. The ratio is 39:8 or about 5:1.
3. You have four outs. The ratio is 43:4 or about 11:1.
4. You have two outs. The ratio is 45:2 or about 23:1.
5. You have 12 outs. The ratio is 35:12 or about 3:1.
6. You have six outs. The ratio is 41:6 or about 7:1.
7. You have 15 outs. The ratio is 32:15 or about 2:1.
8. You have eight outs. The ratio is 39:8 or about 5:1.
9. You have 21 outs. The ratio is 26:21 or about 1.25:1.
10. You have seven outs. The ratio is 40:7 or about 6:1.

Quiz 5

1. $150:$25 or 6:1
2. $55:$5 or 11:1
3. $30:$20 or 1.5:1
4. $475:$100 or 4.75:1
5. $240:$160 or 1.5:1
6. $175:$25 or 7:1
7. $95:$10 or 9.5:1
8. $60:$15 or 4:1
9. $30:$15 or 2:1
10. $180:$60 or 3:1

Quiz 6

1. You have a gutshot straight draw, so you have four outs and are approximately 11:1 against completing on the turn. You must call $10 to win $110, so your pot odds are $110:$10 or 11:1. Since your pot odds are equal to the odds of completing your hand, you are getting sufficient pot odds to call.
2. You have two outs (the other two aces) and are approximately 23:1 against completing on the turn. You must

call $10 to win $260, so your pot odds are $260:$10 or 26:1. Since your pot odds are greater than your odds of completing your hand, you are getting sufficient pot odds to call.

3. You have the nut flush draw, so you have nine outs and are approximately 4:1 against completing on the turn. You must call $60 to win $180, so your pot odds are $180:$60 or 3:1. Since your pot odds are less than your odds of completing your hand, you are getting insufficient pot odds for a call.

4. You have an open-ended straight draw and a flush draw for a total of 15 outs. You are approximately 2:1 against completing on the turn. You must call $120 to win $360, so your pot odds are $360:$120 or 3:1. Since your pot odds are greater than the odds of completing your hand, you are getting sufficient pot odds to call.

5. You have a double gutshot for eight outs and are approximately 5:1 against completing on the turn. You must call $25 to win $135, so your pot odds are $135:$25 or 5.4:1. Since your pot odds are greater than your odds of completing your hand, you are getting sufficient pot odds to call.

6. You have a gutshot straight draw, so you have four outs and are approximately 11:1 against completing on the turn. You must call $15 to win $90, so your pot odds are $90:$15 or 6:1. Since your pot odds are less than your odds of completing your hand, you are getting insufficient pot odds for a call.

7. You have a flush draw and an open-ended straight draw for a total of 15 outs. You are approximately 2:1 against completing on the turn. You must call $20 to win $30, so your pot odds are $30:$20 or 1.5:1. Since your pot odds are less than the odds of completing your hand, you are getting insufficient pot odds to call.

8. You have two overcards only, and assuming they are good you have a total of six outs or are approximately 7:1 against completing on the turn. You must call $5 to win $65, so your pot odds are $65:$5 or 13:1. Since your pot odds are greater than your odds of completing your hand, you are getting sufficient pot odds to call.

9. You have a double gutshot, so you have eight outs and

are approximately 5:1 against hitting your hand on the turn. You must call $40 to win $220, so your pot odds are $220:$40 or 5.5:1. Since your pot odds are greater than the odds of completing your hand, you are getting sufficient pot odds to call.

10. You have two overcards, and assuming they will be good if you hit you have a total of six outs or are approximately 7:1 against completing on the turn. You must call $5 to win $25, so your pot odds are $25:$5 or 5:1. Since your pot odds are less than your odds of completing your hand, you are getting insufficient pot odds to call.

Quiz 7

1. You are 11:1 to make the straight and are getting $130:$50 or less than 3:1 currently. Your typical player, however, isn't going to get off AK in this spot, and his entire $500 is vulnerable. Your implied odds in this case are $630:$50 or almost 13:1; you can call.

2. You are 11:1 to make a straight and are getting $50:$20 or 2.5:1 odds. While your opponent has plenty of chips left, he is a tight player and is unlikely to lose a great deal of chips with one pair. For a call here to be correct, you must be able to collect at least another $170 from him. Fold.

3. You are 5:1 to make the straight and are getting immediate odds of $110:$50 or slightly better than 2:1. The straight possibility isn't well hidden, and your opponent doesn't have that strong a hand. That coupled with his being a timid player reduces the likelihood that you will make much more off him if your card comes. Fold.

4. You are 5:1 to make one of the straights and are getting $65:$25 or about 2.5:1. Because the straight would be hard for an opponent to put you on if you hit, this would be an ideal time to call if she didn't have so few chips left. As it is, even with implied odds, you are being offered only $115:$25 or less than the 5:1 necessary to make a call correct. Fold.

5. You have 10 outs to make either the straight or a set and are about 3.5:1. You are getting 2:1 on a call currently, and though you both have plenty of money left

this wouldn't be a good opportunity to call. Any card that makes your hand makes a very dangerous board, and you can't count on your opponent to make a call. Fold.

6. You are about 7:1 against improving while getting 4:1 currently. While your opponent has enough money left in front of him to make it tempting, it's unlikely that you'll get much more if you hit. All of your outs make his hand obviously vulnerable, and he'd likely muck if you bet the turn if an ace or jack fell. Fold.

7. You are 11:1 against making the straight and are getting $60:$40 or just 1.5:1 on a call. However, your opponent is a loose-aggressive player who will likely be willing to go all-in if you do hit, especially while holding two pair and your straight, if you make it, being difficult to put you on. Therefore, it's reasonable that you could be getting $860:$40 or better than 21:1 on a call. A clear call.

8. This is just a continuation of the previous example. You are about 10.5:1 to make your hand and are getting 2:1 currently with implied odds of 9:1. This is now insufficient to make the call. Fold.

9. You are 11:1 against making the straight and are getting $70:$35 or 2:1 on a call currently. While your opponent has sufficient chips, you can't expect to get too much with three hearts on board. Keep in mind that one of your outs is a Jh, and you are unlikely to get any further money if that card comes, putting four hearts on board. Also, you might make your straight, and then another heart comes on the river, preventing you from collecting even a small bet on that street. Fold.

10. You have 14 outs and are about 2.5:1 to complete your hand. You are getting 2:1 currently but figure on getting sufficient pay from a loose player to justify calling in this spot. Call.

Quiz 8

1. You have top pair with a poor kicker. You are likely beat now, and there are a straight draw and flush draw as well as a number of overcards that could fall — all of which could beat you even if you somehow have the best hand now.

2. The only way you'll get called here is by someone with an ace as well. You can't beat her kicker, and the best that you can hope for is to somehow tie. We don't play poker to get our money back.
3. This hand is eminently playable.
4. We have top pair with a poor kicker. While we are likely beat by the bettor, even if we aren't we can't make any money with such a hand.
5. Let's assume that our opponent is bluffing in this question and has no pair, leaving us with the best possible no pair. So what? Let her win the pot. We can't bet or raise with conviction, and unless an ace or a king falls on the turn we'll have no idea where we are in this hand.
6. Again, we have top pair with a poor kicker. Any card that doesn't pair the board on the turn makes either a straight or a bigger pair. This hand has no potential except for us to get hurt.
7. Besides having a poor kicker with our nine, who will give us any chips without having us beat?
8. We have top pair with a poor kicker and an idiot end straight draw. What do we want to see on the turn? If a six comes and we bet and are raised, then we must muck our hand.
9. This hand should be played.
10. Anyone who calls a bet in this case will have us beat. Check and fold.

Quiz 9

1. You are 39:8 against making your straight on the turn; 39 times you'll lose $15, and eight times you'll win $55. (+$55 x 8) + (-$15 x 39) = -$145/47 = negative EV of $3.09.
2. You are 43:4 against making your straight on the turn; 43 times you'll lose $5, and four times you'll win $35. (+$35 x 4) + (-$5 x 43) = -$75/47 = negative EV of $1.60.
3. You are 43:2 against making your set on the turn (we put our opponent on a set, so we can calculate from 45 unknown cards instead of 47); 43 times you'll lose $0, and two times you'll win $50. (+$50 x $2) + (-$0 x 43) =

$100/45 = positive EV of $2.22.

4. You are 26:21 against improving to the best hand on the turn; 26 times you'll lose $25, and 21 times you'll win $90. (+$90 x 21) + (-$25 x 26) = $1,240/47 = positive EV of $26.38.

5. You are 32:15 against improving to the best hand on the turn; 32 times you'll lose $10, and 15 times you'll win $25. (+$25 x 15) + (-$10 x 32) = $55/47 = positive EV of $1.17.

6. You are 41:6 against improving on the turn; 41 times you'll lose $20, and six times you'll win $60. (+$60 x 6) + (-$20 x 41) = -$460/47 = negative EV of $9.79.

7. You are 39:8 against completing your straight on the turn; 39 times you'll lose $50, and eight times you'll win $140. (+$140 x 8) + (-$50 x 39) = -$830/47 = negative EV of $17.66.

8. You are 43:4 against completing on the turn; 43 times you'll lose $10, and four times you'll win $35. (+$35 x 4) + (-$10 x 43) = -$290/47 = negative EV of $6.17.

9. This is a new situation, but expectation can help us here as well. Twice your opponent won't be bluffing, and you'll lose $50. One time in three, he'll be bluffing, and you'll win $140. (+$140 x 1) + (-$50 x 2) = $40/3 = positive EV of $13.33.

10. Your opponent will be bluffing one time in three, so you'll win $140 one time out of three and lose $90 two times out of three. (+$140 x 1) + (-$90 x 2) = -$40/3 = negative EV of $13.33.

Quiz 10

1. Your opponent has three wins out of 44 unknown cards remaining, which mean you have 41 wins of 44 unknown cards. (41/44)(x/100%) = 93.18%

2. You have eight outs of 44 unknown cards. (8/44)(x/100%) = 18.18%

3. You have four outs of 44 unknown cards. (4/44)(x/100%) = 9.09%

4. Your opponent has 10 outs of 44 unknown cards, leaving you with 34 wins out of 44 unknown cards. (34/44)(x/100%) = 77.27%

5.	Your opponent has no outs, which means you have 100% equity. The math is done the same way.
(44/44)(x/100%) = 100%

6.	This example gets a bit complicated compared to our previous examples. While you can't lose, you can tie. You have nine outs to win, and all other results are ties. (9/44)(x/100) = 20.45%, representing those occasions when you win the entire pot. Of the remaining 79.55%, you have 50% equity or 39.78%. 39.78% + 20.45% = 60.23%

7.	Since both you and your opponent have the same chances of improving to win the entire pot and tying on all other occasions, you have 50% equity.

8.	You have four outs of 44 unknown cards.
(4/44)(x/100%) = 9.09%

9.	You have 12 outs of 44 unknown cards.
(12/44)(x/100%) = 27.27%

10.	You have two outs of 44 unknown cards.
(2/44)(x/100%) = 4.55%

Quiz 11

1.	He thought for a moment and then checked. Why would you do such a thing? Perhaps to get your opponent to think twice before betting. Why wouldn't you want your opponent to bet? Perhaps to get a free card. You wouldn't want a free card if you had a made hand that figured to be the best. If you had a made hand that you weren't sure was the best, you wouldn't want to tip off your opponent that you were unsure by hesitating, would you? If you were unsure that it was the best hand, then you'd have to consider seriously before calling, wouldn't you? The icing on the cake, however, is when he instantly calls. Here's a hand he wasn't sure was good enough to bet, he had to think about whether to bet or not, but he suddenly doesn't have to think to call. He likely has a draw. Since there are two diamonds on the flop and no open-ended straight draws, he likely has the flush draw.

2.	He acted as if he was going to bet, stared you down, and then checked. If we saw this type of bad acting at the movies, we'd walk out. Why would he stare you down before you got to act? He's trying to intimidate you. Why would anyone try to intimidate you if he thought he had the best hand? He wouldn't; he'd invite you to call or bet instead. Also, while I didn't tell you what type of opponent you are facing, it probably isn't a loose-aggressive player. This player raised before the flop and then checked, while any aggressive player would probably bet, let alone a loose-aggressive player. Therefore, when we consider the range of hands that a typical nonaggressive player might raise pre-flop with, we find that the list is pretty short, regardless of position: AA–TT, AKs–Ats, AK–AQ perhaps a few more less likely candidates such as KQ, KJs, and Axs. You can dismiss any hand with an ace in it, which leaves KK–TT and KQ or KJ. He most likely has a big pair; however, your hand is good.

3. Have you ever considered raising pre-flop with AA and then betting in the dark? Of course not; AA is good enough to see a flop with. Often, however, with KK weak players try to appease the poker gods with their show of bravery (i.e., foolhardiness) and try to intimidate their opponents with an incredible show of strength. Don't be impressed; go ahead and call — your hand is good.

4. Typically, when an opponent looks back at her hand, it's because she is hoping she missed something and will find a draw in there. Be careful you don't give this tell away. Your hand is good. There's one more thing to learn from this example, though. If your opponent is capable of giving away such a strong tell, then you should always reach back for chips whether you have any intention of calling or not. If she looks back, then a raise may be in order.

5. The big blind is a very tight player, so what do you think he'll raise to $75 with out of position? As with most tight players, I'd put him on AA or KK, definitely not AK. An ace fell, and he checks. I will bet about $75 here. I will usually bet the size of the pot in situations like this, but my tight opponent won't call me with KK for $75 or for a $150 pot-sized bet. The only way he can call is if he has me beat — in which case I may as well save the $75.

6. There is no trick here; you fold. You are almost certainly beat.

7.   This is a LAP. If he had a raising hand, he wouldn't have been able to contain himself in the first round; he is trying to steal-raise. You have a premium hand and are almost certainly a 2.5:1 or 4:1 favorite (against an Ax or small pair).

8.   The big blind called a substantial bet and a more substantial raise on the flop, immediately indicating a draw. The only reasonable draw on the flop was the JT for an open-ended straight. When the 9s came to make the straight draw good, your opponent checked and then immediately made an effort to show how uninterested he was in the flop by calling for cocktails, encouraging you to bet. Check.

9.   Your opponent almost surely has the straight. You are getting $750:$250 or 3:1 on a call, and he is making it enticing. Don't fall for it; you should fold unless you can be certain there is a one-in-four chance or better that he doesn't have the straight. Since the hand was played, there's significantly less chance that this is the case. Fold.

10. This is a good player who raised in early position, indicating a strong hand. A likely range is AA, KK, QQ, JJ, AK, or AQ. You raised and were called. The flop came all undercards, and he bet. He knows you have a hand as well, yet he bet into you. This is likely not an AK or AQ. He has a big pair. You can tie with JJ and lose to every other possible hand. Fold.

Appendix B

Rank	10-Handed 10.00	9-Handed 11.11	8-Handed 12.50	7-Handed 14.29	6-Handed 16.67	5-Handed 20.00	4-Handed 25.00	3-Handed 33.33	Heads-Up 50.00
AA	31.06	34.70	38.66	43.50	49.24	55.79	63.87	73.42	85.25
KK	26.09	29.18	32.91	37.42	43.01	49.79	58.18	68.95	82.42
QQ	22.30	24.89	28.35	32.55	37.90	44.71	53.55	64.96	79.93
AKs	20.67	22.70	25.05	27.65	31.06	35.38	41.41	50.61	67.00
JJ	19.37	21.68	24.65	28.55	33.57	40.31	49.13	61.21	77.45
AQs	19.29	21.19	23.30	25.94	29.25	33.66	39.84	49.50	66.25
KQs	18.61	20.34	22.54	25.19	28.31	32.46	38.10	47.07	63.43
AJs	18.16	19.82	22.04	24.69	27.94	32.22	38.51	48.33	65.43
KJs	17.64	19.32	21.42	23.82	27.03	31.02	36.82	45.81	62.50
ATs	17.34	18.97	21.06	23.51	26.70	31.08	37.21	47.00	64.82
TT	17.22	19.15	21.81	25.28	29.98	36.35	45.27	57.58	75.03
AK	17.19	19.22	21.58	24.45	27.89	32.31	38.49	48.17	65.26
QJs	17.10	18.72	20.79	23.17	26.31	30.16	35.68	44.07	60.22
KTs	16.88	18.43	20.45	22.91	25.86	29.89	35.65	44.80	61.79
JTs	16.65	18.01	19.75	22.01	24.91	28.62	33.89	41.94	57.51
QTs	16.46	14.47	19.92	22.20	25.22	29.06	34.56	43.17	59.44
99	15.59	17.20	19.44	22.45	26.58	32.65	41.17	53.67	72.05
AQ	15.54	17.54	19.67	22.48	25.91	30.48	36.83	46.69	64.47
A9s	15.30	16.97	18.73	21.03	24.19	28.34	34.57	44.56	62.75
KQ	15.13	16.97	19.08	21.70	25.08	29.23	35.10	44.39	61.47
K9s	14.85	16.40	18.20	20.34	23.25	27.19	32.86	42.20	60.01
A8s	14.73	16.22	18.04	20.22	23.20	27.41	33.48	43.46	61.93
Q9s	14.72	15.90	17.60	19.87	22.51	26.49	31.82	40.67	57.62

Rank	10-Handed 10.00	9-Handed 11.11	8-Handed 12.50	7-Handed 14.29	6-Handed 16.67	5-Handed 20.00	4-Handed 25.00	3-Handed 33.33	Heads-Up 50.00
J9s	14.51	15.91	17.57	19.67	22.42	26.01	31.22	39.41	55.75
88	14.47	15.86	17.76	20.37	23.97	29.49	37.57	49.99	69.14
A5s	14.41	15.82	17.46	19.55	22.21	25.96	31.68	41.38	59.90
A7s	14.32	15.63	17.33	19.54	22.39	26.41	32.42	42.38	61.00
AJ	14.30	16.06	18.30	21.05	24.35	28.83	35.28	45.48	63.47
A6s	14.21	15.32	16.78	18.89	21.64	25.46	31.31	41.16	59.85
A4s	14.19	15.49	17.04	19.11	21.64	25.35	30.99	40.49	59.06
T9s	14.08	16.07	17.73	19.75	22.40	26.04	30.99	38.73	54.04
A3s	14.01	15.16	16.73	18.67	21.16	24.76	30.30	39.64	58.23
KJ	13.98	15.64	17.72	20.33	23.53	27.73	33.70	43.13	60.64
77	13.68	14.80	16.41	18.63	21.93	26.81	34.36	46.45	66.26
QJ	13.66	15.39	17.35	19.83	22.95	26.95	32.57	41.22	58.09
A2s	13.63	14.70	16.25	18.16	20.62	24.13	29.43	38.85	57.42
K8s	13.56	14.92	16.53	18.68	21.43	25.12	30.77	40.24	58.41
AT	13.38	15.09	21.06	19.70	23.06	27.58	34.05	44.26	62.72
98s	13.32	14.56	15.99	17.80	20.22	23.64	28.52	35.91	50.82
J8s	13.21	14.44	15.99	17.97	20.45	23.99	29.05	37.49	54.04
Q8s	13.16	14.44	16.07	18.06	20.78	24.40	29.73	38.50	55.97
K7s	13.15	14.36	16.00	18.02	20.73	24.39	29.96	39.17	57.59
JT	13.11	14.57	16.33	18.59	21.47	25.41	30.67	41.94	55.25
66	13.07	13.96	15.43	17.27	20.08	24.44	31.44	43.33	63.27
T8s	13.05	14.74	16.25	18.06	20.58	24.00	28.86	36.70	52.36
KT	13.00	14.78	16.71	19.19	22.26	26.45	32.42	41.84	59.81
QT	12.95	14.47	16.41	18.69	21.66	25.72	31.39	40.19	57.29
K6s	12.88	14.04	15.48	17.55	20.02	23.54	25.25	38.36	56.68

Rank	10-Handed 10.00	9-Handed 11.11	8-Handed 12.50	7-Handed 14.29	6-Handed 16.67	5-Handed 20.00	4-Handed 25.00	3-Handed 33.33	Heads-Up 50.00
87s	12.85	13.73	15.07	16.81	18.99	22.10	26.62	33.75	47.96
K5s	12.54	13.67	15.21	17.05	19.52	22.98	28.23	37.20	55.75
97s	12.54	13.50	14.95	16.66	18.85	21.95	26.68	34.11	49.16
76s	12.37	13.31	14.40	15.95	17.90	20.79	25.09	31.94	45.30
55	12.37	13.24	14.41	16.08	18.52	22.45	28.93	40.03	60.32
K4s	12.34	13.43	14.85	16.60	19.00	22.40	27.42	36.65	54.83
T7s	12.29	13.35	14.83	16.51	18.91	22.13	26.97	34.67	50.57
44	12.17	12.85	13.97	15.21	17.36	20.64	26.27	36.84	56.95
Q7s	12.15	13.29	14.70	16.59	19.04	22.51	27.72	36.44	54.30
K3s	12.13	13.25	14.65	16.32	18.70	21.86	26.86	35.73	54.08
33	12.00	12.69	13.49	14.75	16.27	19.13	24.03	33.62	53.67
J7s	12.00	13.15	14.66	16.42	18.84	22.23	27.11	35.39	52.29
22	11.96	12.55	13.16	14.16	15.52	17.73	21.89	30.70	50.40
86s	11.95	12.89	14.05	15.64	17.71	20.63	24.97	31.93	46.28
65s	11.93	12.74	13.84	15.18	17.07	19.67	23.67	30.22	43.08
K2s	11.92	13.05	14.31	16.02	18.25	21.33	26.22	34.97	53.14
Q6s	11.80	12.86	14.29	16.04	18.48	21.91	27.06	35.78	53.59
54s	11.67	12.58	13.53	14.78	16.44	18.92	22.71	28.94	41.42
Q5s	11.59	12.63	13.97	15.81	18.03	21.24	26.26	34.84	52.85
96s	11.44	12.42	13.54	15.15	17.47	20.36	24.87	32.10	47.43
75s	11.41	12.37	13.43	14.80	16.74	19.43	23.40	30.19	43.68
Q4s	11.31	12.32	13.72	15.38	17.58	20.73	25.56	34.05	51.80
T9	11.25	12.63	14.16	16.14	18.84	22.55	27.60	35.69	51.46
A9	11.16	12.69	14.73	17.02	20.20	24.60	30.98	41.61	60.80
T6s	11.16	12.21	13.55	15.19	17.35	20.45	25.02	32.82	48.96

Rank	10-Handed 10.00	9-Handed 11.11	8-Handed 12.50	7-Handed 14.29	6-Handed 16.67	5-Handed 20.00	4-Handed 25.00	3-Handed 33.33	Heads-Up 50.00
64s	11.15	11.90	12.94	14.22	15.82	18.43	22.22	28.51	41.38
Q3s	11.11	12.11	13.46	15.05	17.11	20.25	24.95	33.25	51.08
Q2s	11.08	11.94	13.21	14.75	16.87	19.72	24.26	32.38	50.12
J6s	11.07	12.06	13.42	15.08	17.37	20.45	25.24	33.34	50.59
J9	10.96	12.17	13.84	16.11	18.77	22.53	27.85	36.36	53.22
K9	10.90	12.26	14.13	16.37	19.48	23.59	29.52	39.38	57.83
85s	10.90	11.84	12.88	14.25	16.32	19.06	23.22	30.08	44.64
53s	10.90	11.61	12.55	13.78	15.40	17.61	21.14	27.21	39.74
J5s	10.81	11.82	13.14	14.76	16.90	20.01	24.67	32.66	50.08
J4s	10.77	11.56	12.83	14.42	16.50	19.46	23.99	31.89	49.06
Q9	10.75	12.07	13.81	16.03	18.87	22.81	28.46	37.49	55.35
A8	10.53	11.94	13.76	16.14	19.20	23.56	29.96	40.36	59.87
74s	10.45	11.22	12.31	13.55	15.42	17.92	21.81	28.26	41.83
95s	10.39	11.29	12.47	13.87	15.93	18.79	23.05	30.26	45.69
J3s	10.38	11.41	12.49	14.04	16.21	18.89	23.32	31.25	48.16
J2s	10.35	11.17	12.38	13.74	15.64	18.48	22.73	30.32	47.44
43s	10.32	11.21	12.07	13.25	14.79	16.89	20.41	26.45	38.72
T5s	10.31	11.18	12.35	13.91	15.95	18.94	23.24	30.73	47.17
63s	10.09	10.81	11.84	13.02	14.60	16.83	20.44	26.69	36.20
T4s	10.05	10.94	12.15	13.58	15.62	18.38	22.70	30.17	46.52
A5	10.05	11.41	13.11	15.18	18.10	21.97	27.97	38.20	57.75
A7	9.93	11.39	13.04	15.29	18.32	22.45	28.72	39.18	58.78
T8	9.92	11.00	12.45	14.42	16.94	20.38	25.41	33.55	49.74
T3s	9.92	10.83	11.91	13.33	15.20	17.94	22.11	29.44	45.81
A4	9.85	11.11	12.68	14.75	17.50	21.37	27.10	37.18	56.81

Rank	10-Handed 10.00	9-Handed 11.11	8-Handed 12.50	7-Handed 14.29	6-Handed 16.67	5-Handed 20.00	4-Handed 25.00	3-Handed 33.33	Heads-Up 50.00
52s	9.85	10.63	11.50	12.63	14.09	16.19	19.50	25.41	41.09
84s	9.82	10.78	11.71	13.12	14.89	17.51	21.49	28.27	43.41
T2s	9.75	10.60	11.72	13.09	14.91	17.51	21.48	28.73	43.52
42s	9.71	10.30	11.19	12.26	13.63	15.61	18.83	24.73	40.47
A6	9.55	10.85	12.48	14.64	17.46	21.38	27.58	37.88	57.95
A3	9.55	10.76	12.38	14.34	16.97	20.62	26.31	36.44	56.54
J8	9.50	10.62	12.16	14.11	16.81	20.30	25.59	34.22	47.79
K8	9.43	10.73	12.45	14.62	17.49	21.30	27.07	37.01	52.87
87	9.29	10.13	11.44	13.01	15.30	18.39	23.09	30.50	45.12
94s	9.24	10.31	11.37	12.72	14.64	17.26	17.33	28.25	43.56
A2	9.21	10.36	11.93	13.81	16.32	19.91	25.46	35.19	56.35
Q8	9.18	10.55	12.08	14.11	16.87	20.59	26.17	35.16	49.42
32s	9.15	9.90	10.63	11.62	13.11	15.03	18.22	23.94	39.91
93s	9.15	10.15	11.14	12.49	14.31	16.92	20.93	27.87	46.40
92s	9.12	9.95	10.95	12.23	13.91	16.46	20.27	27.07	42.74
98	9.08	10.94	12.32	14.11	16.73	20.08	25.03	32.68	46.24
62s	9.05	9.76	10.66	11.75	13.33	15.40	18.84	24.84	41.36
73s	9.04	10.22	11.11	12.40	14.01	16.40	20.04	26.33	42.43
83s	8.96	9.75	10.72	11.98	13.65	16.08	19.74	26.36	42.50
K7	8.95	10.14	11.80	13.81	16.70	20.52	26.18	36.00	58.15
76	8.83	9.58	10.67	12.14	14.13	17.11	21.38	28.40	42.26
97	8.83	9.81	11.13	12.84	15.14	18.33	23.14	30.54	46.36
82s	8.79	9.55	10.54	11.76	13.31	15.71	19.35	25.91	40.18
T7	8.57	9.56	10.98	12.75	15.12	18.34	23.24	31.27	47.90
K6	8.56	9.76	11.34	13.33	15.96	19.56	25.36	34.99	54.23

Rank	10-Handed 10.00	9-Handed 11.11	8-Handed 12.50	7-Handed 14.29	6-Handed 16.67	5-Handed 20.00	4-Handed 25.00	3-Handed 33.33	Heads-Up 50.00
72s	8.52	9.29	10.21	11.31	12.87	15.03	18.50	24.62	38.23
65	8.43	9.23	10.14	11.47	13.30	15.90	19.91	26.60	39.92
86	8.31	9.07	10.30	11.79	13.85	16.82	21.19	28.46	43.27
K5	8.26	9.45	10.91	12.79	15.35	18.93	24.46	33.97	53.43
54	8.24	8.94	9.81	10.99	12.65	15.08	18.89	25.35	38.06
J7	8.12	9.18	10.67	12.45	14.87	18.32	23.41	31.88	49.72
K4	8.03	9.20	10.52	12.30	14.76	18.25	23.62	33.05	52.37
Q7	8.03	9.22	10.63	12.54	15.07	18.58	23.87	33.14	51.68
K3	7.88	8.95	10.24	12.05	14.30	17.63	22.86	32.04	51.34
75	7.88	8.67	9.72	11.01	12.90	15.56	19.62	26.49	40.57
96	7.75	8.62	9.73	11.38	13.40	16.50	21.08	28.62	44.57
Q6	7.73	8.81	10.19	11.98	14.45	17.83	23.09	32.23	50.97
K2	7.66	8.68	10.00	11.59	13.89	17.02	22.01	31.18	50.61
64	7.60	8.30	9.17	10.40	12.03	14.46	18.28	24.65	38.04
53	7.45	8.07	8.85	9.90	11.46	13.68	17.22	23.59	36.26
Q5	7.36	8.43	9.80	11.49	13.91	17.22	22.33	31.35	50.14
T6	7.31	8.26	9.61	11.23	13.43	16.48	21.16	29.15	46.04
85	7.15	8.04	9.01	10.41	12.41	15.10	19.32	26.48	41.41
Q4	7.10	8.19	9.48	11.06	13.36	16.63	21.59	30.35	49.19
J6	6.99	8.05	9.37	11.05	13.27	16.43	21.36	29.77	47.81
Q3	6.94	7.94	9.13	10.73	12.93	16.04	20.78	29.58	48.20
43	6.88	7.56	8.31	9.30	10.74	12.90	16.37	22.44	35.29
J5	6.87	7.74	8.96	10.65	12.76	15.98	20.72	29.05	47.03
Q2	6.86	7.77	8.88	10.39	12.48	15.48	20.12	28.74	47.28
74	6.85	7.57	8.49	9.71	11.42	13.89	17.83	24.48	38.62

Rank	10-Handed 10.00	9-Handed 11.11	8-Handed 12.50	7-Handed 14.29	6-Handed 16.67	5-Handed 20.00	4-Handed 25.00	3-Handed 33.33	Heads-Up 50.00
J4	6.63	7.49	8.69	10.19	12.25	15.30	19.99	28.16	46.12
95	6.53	7.45	8.48	9.93	11.95	14.81	19.15	26.54	42.76
T5	6.46	7.21	8.37	9.85	11.89	14.82	19.34	27.17	44.34
J3	6.38	7.30	8.41	9.80	11.86	14.73	19.30	27.41	45.28
63	6.38	7.12	7.95	9.03	10.54	12.85	16.49	22.81	35.88
52	6.36	6.94	7.70	8.63	10.00	12.10	15.42	21.40	34.34
J2	6.25	7.11	8.17	9.52	11.39	14.27	18.62	26.45	44.44
T4	6.17	6.96	8.08	9.50	11.48	14.29	18.75	26.45	43.47
84	6.13	6.85	7.76	9.08	10.84	13.47	17.48	24.39	39.36
T3	6.04	6.70	7.80	9.17	11.09	13.81	17.99	25.57	42.52
42	6.04	6.61	7.31	8.27	9.56	11.56	14.74	20.66	33.22
T2	5.83	6.52	7.54	8.92	10.68	13.19	17.31	24.78	41.68
73	5.72	6.43	7.26	8.40	9.93	12.30	16.01	22.47	36.62
94	5.64	6.35	7.36	8.70	10.49	13.15	17.29	24.62	40.61
32	5.61	6.11	6.87	7.72	8.96	10.82	13.95	19.90	32.30
93	5.44	6.17	7.06	8.36	10.14	12.72	16.76	23.96	40.00
62	5.40	6.03	6.78	7.76	9.91	11.26	14.69	20.84	33.88
92	5.23	5.97	6.88	8.12	9.74	12.19	16.08	23.16	39.06
83	5.18	5.82	6.74	7.86	9.49	11.88	15.63	22.52	37.58
82	4.95	5.71	6.47	7.51	9.18	11.55	15.18	21.82	37.09
72	4.80	5.41	6.20	7.18	8.64	10.77	14.21	20.56	34.54

Appendix C

Rank	10-Handed 10.00	9-Handed 11.11	8-Handed 12.50	7-Handed 14.29	6-Handed 16.67	5-Handed 20.00	4-Handed 25.00	3-Handed 33.33	Heads-Up 50.00
1.	AA	AA	AA	AA	AA	AA	AA	AA	AA
2.	KK	KK	KK	KK	KK	KK	KK	KK	KK
3.	QQ	QQ	QQ	QQ	QQ	QQ	QQ	QQ	QQ
4.	AKs	AKs	AKs	JJ	AKs	JJ	JJ	JJ	JJ
5.	JJ	JJ	JJ	AKs	JJ	TT	TT	TT	TT
6.	AQs	AQs	AQs	AQs	TT	AKs	AKs	99	99
7.	KQs	KQs	KQs	TT	AQs	AQs	99	AKs	88
8.	AJs	AJs	AJs	KQs	KQs	99	AQs	88	AKs
9.	KJs	KJs	TT	AJs	AJs	KQs	AJs	AQs	77
10.	ATs	AK	AK	AK	AK	AK	AK	AJs	AQs
11.	TT	TT	KJs	KJs	KJs	AJs	KQs	AK	AJs
12.	AK	ATs	ATs	ATs	ATs	ATs	88	KQs	AK
13.	QJs	QJs	AT	QJs	99	KJs	ATs	ATs	ATs
14.	KTs	KTs	QJs	KTs	QJs	AQ	AQ	AQ	AQ
15.	JTs	JTs	KTs	AQ	QJs	QJs	KJs	77	AJ
16.	QTs	AQ	QTs	99	KTs	KTs	QJs	KJs	KQs
17.	99	99	JTs	QTs	QTs	88	KTs	AJ	66
18.	AQ	A9s	AQ	JTs	KQ	KQ	AJ	KTs	A9s
19.	A9s	KQ	99	KQ	JTs	QTs	KQ	A9s	AT
20.	KQ	K9s	KQ	AJ	AJ	AJ	A9s	KQ	KJs
21.	K9s	A8s	A9s	A9s	A9s	JTs	QTs	AT	A8s
22.	A8s	T9s	AJ	88	88	A9s	77	QJs	KTs
23.	Q9s	AJ	K9s	K9s	KJ	KJ	AT	A8s	KQ

Rank	10-Handed 10.00	9-Handed 11.11	8-Handed 12.50	7-Handed 14.29	6-Handed 16.67	5-Handed 20.00	4-Handed 25.00	3-Handed 33.33	Heads-Up 50.00
24.	J9s	J9s	A8s	KJ	K9s	AT	JTs	66	A7s
25.	88	Q9s	88	A8s	A8s	A8s	KJ	QTs	A9
26.	A5s	88	T9s	Q9s	AT	K9s	A8s	KJ	KJ
27.	A7s	A5s	KJ	QJ	QJ	QJ	K9s	A7s	55
28.	AJ	KJ	Q9s	T9s	Q9s	77	QJ	K9s	QJs
29.	A6s	A7s	J9s	AT	J9s	Q9s	A7s	JTs	K9s
30.	A4s	A4s	A5s	J9s	T9s	KT	KT	JT	A5s
31.	T9s	QJ	QJ	A5s	A7s	A7s	Q9s	KT	A8
32.	A3s	A6s	A7s	A7s	KT	T9s	A5s	A9	A6s
33.	KJ	A3s	A4s	KT	A5s	J9s	66	A5s	KT
34.	77	AT	A6s	A4s	77	A5s	QT	QJ	QTs
35.	QJ	K8s	A3s	A6s	QT	QT	A6s	A6s	A4s
36.	A2s	77	KT	QT	A6s	A6s	J9s	Q9s	A7
37.	K8s	KT	K8s	K8s	A4s	JT	A4s	A4s	K8s
38.	AT	T8s	77	A3s	JT	A4s	T9s	A8	A3s
39.	98s	A2s	QT	77	K8s	K8s	A9	K8s	K7
40.	J8s	JT	JT	JT	A3s	A3s	K8s	QT	QJ
41.	Q8s	98s	A2s	A2s	Q8s	A9	JT	55	A6
42.	K7s	QTs	T8s	Q8s	K7s	66	A3s	A3s	K9
43.	JT	QT	Q8s	T8s	A2s	Q8s	K7s	J9s	A5
44.	66	J8s	K7s	K7s	T8s	K7s	A8	K9	Q9s
45.	T8s	Q8s	98s	J8s	J8s	A2s	Q8s	A7	K7s
46.	KT	K7s	J8s	98s	98s	T8s	K9	K7s	JTs
47.	QT	K6s	K6s	K6s	A9	J8s	A2s	A2s	A2s
48.	K6s	66	66	66	66	98s	J8s	T9s	QT

Rank	10-Handed 10.00	9-Handed 11.11	8-Handed 12.50	7-Handed 14.29	6-Handed 16.67	5-Handed 20.00	4-Handed 25.00	3-Handed 33.33	Heads-Up 50.00
49.	87s	87s	K5s	K5s	K6s	K9	55	Q8s	44
50.	K5s	K5s	87s	A9	K5s	A8	T8s	K6s	A4
51.	97s	97s	97s	87s	K9	K6s	A7	A5	K6s
52.	76s	K4s	K4s	97s	A8	K5s	98s	A6	A3
53.	55	T7s	T7s	K4s	Q7s	Q9	Q9	J8s	A2
54.	K4s	76s	A9	Q7s	K4s	T9	K5s	Q9	Q8s
55.	T7s	Q7s	Q7s	T7s	87s	J9	A5	K5s	J9s
56.	44	K3s	J7s	J7s	T7s	Q7s	J9	A4	K5s
57.	Q7s	55	K3s	K9	Q9	55	Q7s	K8	Q9
58.	K3s	J7s	55	K3s	97s	A7	T9	44	JT
59.	33	K2s	76s	T9	T9	K4s	A6	T8s	K4s
60.	J7s	86s	K2s	A8	J7s	J7s	K4s	K4s	Q7s
61.	22	Q6s	Q6s	J9	J9	T7s	J7s	Q7s	K6
62.	86s	44	T9	55	K3s	87s	A4	A3	K3s
63.	65s	65s	K9	Q6s	55	A5	K8	J9	T9s
64.	K2s	33	86s	Q9	Q6s	97s	Q6s	K7	J8s
65.	Q6s	A9	44	K2s	A7	Q6s	T7s	98s	33
66.	54s	Q5s	Q5s	76s	K2s	K3s	K3s	Q6s	Q6s
67.	Q5s	T9	65s	Q5s	A5	A6	97s	K3s	K5
68.	96s	54s	J9	86s	Q5s	A4	87s	T9	J9
69.	75s	22	Q9	Q4s	76s	K2s	A3	J7s	K2s
70.	Q4s	96s	A8	A7	86s	K8	44	A2	K8
71.	T9	75s	Q4s	44	Q4s	Q5s	Q5s	Q8	Q5s
72.	A9	Q4s	T6s	T6s	A4	76s	K2s	K6	K4
73.	T6s	K9	96s	65s	K8	Q4s	K7	K2s	T8s

Rank	10-Handed 10.00	9-Handed 11.11	8-Handed 12.50	7-Handed 14.29	6-Handed 16.67	5-Handed 20.00	4-Handed 25.00	3-Handed 33.33	Heads-Up 50.00
74.	64s	T6s	54s	A5	96s	44	Q8	Q5s	J7s
75.	Q3s	J9	33	96s	A6	86s	J8	T7s	Q4s
76.	Q2s	Q3s	Q3s	J6s	J6s	A3	Q4s	J8	Q7
77.	J6s	Q9	75s	Q3s	44	Q8	A2	97s	T9
78.	J9	J6s	J6s	75s	T6s	K7	T8	Q4s	K3
79.	K9	Q2s	Q2s	54s	Q3s	T6s	K6	K5	Q3s
80.	85s	A8	22	J5s	65s	J6s	K6s	87s	Q6
81.	53s	64s	J5s	33	A3	T8	J6s	33	98s
82.	J5s	85s	A5	Q2s	T8	96s	76s	T8	K2
83.	J4s	J5s	A7	A4	J5s	J8	98	J6s	J6s
84.	Q9	53s	64s	A6	Q8	Q3s	T6s	Q3s	T7s
85.	A8	J4s	85s	K8	Q2s	98	86s	Q7	22
86.	74s	J3s	J4s	J4s	J8	J5s	Q3s	K4	Q5
87.	95s	A5	A4	T8	75s	A2	96s	T6s	Q2s
88.	J3s	A7	53s	A3	98	Q2s	J5s	98	J5s
89.	J2s	95s	J3s	85s	K7	65s	K5	J5s	T8
90.	43s	74s	A6	64s	J4s	K6	Q2s	Q2s	J7
91.	T5s	43s	95s	22	54s	J4s	33	Q6	Q8
92.	63s	T5s	T8	J8	A2	75s	J4s	96s	Q4
93.	T4s	J2s	K8	Q8	85s	33	Q7	K3	97s
94.	A5	A4	J2s	98	33	85s	65s	76s	J4s
95.	A7	T8	A3	J3s	J3s	T5s	K4	86s	T6s
96.	T8	T4s	T5s	T5s	K6	K5	J7	J4s	Q3
97.	T3s	98	98	95s	T5s	54s	75s	J7	J3s
98.	A4	A6	74s	A2	95s	J3s	J3s	Q5	87s

Rank	10-Handed 10.00	9-Handed 11.11	8-Handed 12.50	7-Handed 14.29	6-Handed 16.67	5-Handed 20.00	4-Handed 25.00	3-Handed 33.33	Heads-Up 50.00
99.	52s	T3s	J8	K7	64s	95s	T5s	T7	T7
100.	84s	63s	T4s	53s	J2s	Q7	T7	J3s	J6
101.	T2s	84s	Q8	J2s	T4s	J2s	85s	K2	J8
102.	42s	A3	43s	T4s	22	64s	97	T5s	J2s
103.	A6	K8	A2	74s	74s	87	87	22	96s
104.	A3	52s	T3s	T3s	53s	T4s	Q6	97	Q2
105.	J8	J8	63s	K6	K5	T7	95s	87	T5s
106.	K8	T2s	K7	43s	87	97	K3	Q4	J5
107.	87	Q8	T2s	84s	T3s	J7	J2s	J2s	T4s
108.	94s	A2	84s	T2s	97	K4	54s	95s	93s
109.	A2	94s	52s	63s	T7	T3s	T4s	65s	97
110.	Q8	42s	87	87	Q7	74s	Q5	75s	86s
111.	32s	73s	94s	97	T2s	Q6	64s	T4s	98
112.	93s	93s	K6	K5	84s	22	T3s	85s	J4
113.	92s	K7	42s	T7	J7	K3	K2	J6	T6
114.	98	87	93s	94s	43s	53s	22	Q3	T3s
115.	62s	92s	97	52s	K4	84s	74s	T3s	95s
116.	73s	32s	73s	Q7	94s	T2s	Q4	T6	76s
117.	83s	97	T7	93s	63s	94s	84s	J5	J3
118.	K7	62s	92s	J7	Q6	Q5	T2s	54s	87
119.	76	K6	K5	73s	93s	76	76	Q2	85s
120.	97	83s	83s	K4	K3	K2	J6	T2s	96
121.	82s	76	76	42s	76	93s	86	96	J2
122.	T7	T7	J7	92s	52s	43s	T6	64s	T5
123.	K6	82s	62s	76	73s	63s	53s	86	75s

Rank	10-Handed 10.00	9-Handed 11.11	8-Handed 12.50	7-Handed 14.29	6-Handed 16.67	5-Handed 20.00	4-Handed 25.00	3-Handed 33.33	Heads-Up 50.00
124.	72s	K5	32s	K3	Q5	86	96	76	94s
125.	65	72s	Q7	83s	92s	Q4	93s	84s	T2s
126.	86	65	82s	Q6	K2	96	Q3	74s	T4
127.	K5	Q7	K4	86	86	T6	J5	94s	84s
128.	54	K4	86	82s	83s	92s	63s	J4	86
129.	J7	J7	K3	62s	42s	J6	43s	93s	65s
130.	K4	86	72s	32s	T6	73s	92s	J3	95
131.	Q7	K3	Q6	K2	96	52s	Q2	53s	92s
132.	K3	54	65	Q5	Q4	83s	73s	T5	T3
133.	75	Q6	K2	65	62s	Q3	J4	92s	83s
134.	96	K2	54	96	82s	J5	65	63s	73s
135.	Q6	75	Q5	72s	65	65	83s	65	76
136.	K2	96	96	T6	J6	82s	75	95	74s
137.	64	Q5	75	Q4	32s	42s	52s	75	T2
138.	53	64	T6	J6	Q3	75	82s	85	54s
139.	Q5	T6	Q4	75	75	Q2	T5	43s	85
140.	T6	Q4	J6	54	72s	62s	85	J2	64s
141.	85	53	64	Q3	J5	J4	J3	T4	62s
142.	Q4	J6	Q3	J5	54	85	95	83s	52s
143.	J6	85	85	85	Q2	54	54	73s	94
144.	Q3	Q3	J5	64	85	32s	62s	82s	75
145.	43	Q2	Q2	Q2	J4	72s	42s	T3	42s
146.	J5	J5	53	J4	64	T5	T4	52s	82s
147.	Q2	74	J4	95	95	95	J2	54	93
148.	74	43	74	53	T5	J3	72s	62s	65

Rank	10-Handed 10.00	9-Handed 11.11	8-Handed 12.50	7-Handed 14.29	6-Handed 16.67	5-Handed 20.00	4-Handed 25.00	3-Handed 33.33	Heads-Up 50.00
149.	J4	J4	95	T5	J3	64	64	T2	32s
150.	95	95	J3	J3	T4	T4	32s	42s	53s
151.	T5	J3	T5	74	53	J2	T3	64	84
152.	J3	T5	43	J2	74	74	74	72s	92
153.	63	63	J2	T4	J2	T3	84	94	43s
154.	52	J2	T4	43	T3	53	94s	74	74
155.	J2	T4	63	T3	84	84	T2	84	72s
156.	T4	52	T3	84	43	T2	94	93	54
157.	84	84	84	63	T2	94	53	32s	64
158.	T3	T3	52	T2	63	43	93	53	83
159.	42	42	T2	94	94	63	63	92	82
160.	T2	T2	94	52	93	93	43	63	73
161.	73	73	42	73	52	73	92	83	53
162.	94	94	73	93	73	92	73	73	63s
163.	32	93	93	42	62	52	83	43	63
164.	93	32	92	92	92	83	52	82	43
165.	62	62	32	83	42	42	82	52	72
166.	92	92	62	62	83	82	42	62	52
167.	83	83	83	32	82	62	62	42	62
168.	82	82	82	82	32	32	72	72	42
169.	72	72	72	72	72	72	32	32	32